THE VATICAN CHRISTMAS COOKBOOK

The Vatican Christmas Cookbook

Contributing Authors
David Geisser & Thomas Kelly

Photographs
All photographs by Roy Matter, except as noted on page 177.

Translations
Archangel Press

Supervising Editor
Thomas Kelly

Editorial Consultant
Dan O'Shannon

Editors
Angie Allen
Sue Allen
Alexa Simmons

IT & Graphic Director
Michael Criscione

Cover and Interior Design
Perceptions Design Studio

Image Processing
Vista Productions

Production Consultant
Thomas Wilson

Recipe & Culinary Advisor
Selina Geisser

Photography & Image Supervisor
Julianna Walborn

Legal & Copyrights
Harold Pollock

Swiss Guard & Vatican Liaison
Andreas Widmer

SOPHIA
INSTITUTE PRESS

Sophia Institute Press®
Box 5284, Manchester, NH 03108
1-800-888-9344

www.SophiaInstitute.com
Sophia Institute Press® is a registered trademark of Sophia Institute.

ISBN: 978-1-64413-305-7

Library of Congress Control Number:
9781644133057

THE
VATICAN
Christmas
COOKBOOK

DAVID GEISSER &
THOMAS KELLY

FIRST EDITION

SOPHIA INSTITUTE PRESS
Manchester, New Hampshire

⚔ CONTENTS

Dedication vii
Foreword ix
Introduction xi

Advent 1
The Coming of the Guard 5
Hearty Barley Soup 7
Apple Bread 9
Pumpkin Soup Amaretto 11
Saint Nicholas 13
Little Santas 15

Christmas Eve 17
Papalin Fettuccine 19
Pizza Raclette 21
Lasagna Bolognese 23
Polish Borscht 25

Christmas 29
Stuffed Chicken Breast with Peppers 33
Veal Tartare in Truffle Oil 35
Filet Mignon with Racy Pepper Sauce 37
The History of Christmas 39
Pork Tenderloin in Puff Pastry 41
Lamb with Herb Crust & Mediterranean Vegetables 43
Venison in Fig Sauce 45
Tagliatelle Porcini 47
Christmas at the Vatican 49
Muggi's Mincemeat 53
Roasted Trout with Fennel and Baguette 55
Veal Chanterelle 57
Beef Rib Mediterranean 59
Caponata Gamberoni 61
Swiss Guard Christmas Watch 63
Roast Christmas Turkey 67
Egg Williams Soufflé 71
Ricotta Lemon Ravioli 73

Salmon Club Sandwich 75
Linguine Carbonara 77

Dishes on the Side 78
  Lemon Rice 79
  Champagne Risotto 79
  Potatoes au Gratin 79
  Polenta au Gratin 80
  Mashed Floury Potatoes 80
  Pea Mashed Potatoes 81
  Potato Balls 81
  Beet Risotto 84
  Rosemary Potatoes 84
  German Potato Salad 85
  Poppyseed Spaetzle 85
  Nudge Noodle 86
  Truffle Risotto 86
  Rösti 87
  Saffron Risotto 87

The Joy of Fondue 88
  Vaud Fondue 89
  Fondue Moitié-Moitié 90
  Geneva Fondue 91
  Tilsit Red Fondue 92
  Tomato Fondue 93

Christmas with the Popes **95**
Pope Saint Leo the Great: Christmas 451 96
Pope Gregory: Christmas 592 98
Pope Benedict XV: Christmas 1919 99
Pope Saint John Paul II: Christmas 1981 102

Christmas Desserts & Cookies **107**
Maple Cream Cake 109
Gingerbread Plum Parfait 111
Clafouti 113
Chocolate Cake Surprise 115

Cheesecake David 117
Dark Toblerone Mousse. 119
Pistachio Torrone. 121
Chocolate Almond Cookies. 125
Apricot Jewels. 127
Lemon Sugar Cookies. 129
Cinnamon Stars 131
Anisettes. 133
Hazelnut Cookies 135
Sables 137
Amaretti 139
Vanilla Almond Cookies 141
Christmas Prayers & Graces. 142

Christmas Around the World **145**
Argentina: Feliz Navidad 146
Egypt: Eid Milad Majid. 147
The Philippines: Maligayang Pasko 148
Switzerland: Schöni Wiehnachte. 149
Fondue Chinoise. 151
Duck with Cranberry Sauce. 153
Spinach Potato Gnocchi. 155
Rabbit Mezze 157
Fajitas Argentine. 159
Tajine Beef & Couscous Salad. 161

Epiphany **163**
The Three Wise Men 167
Dal 169
Tajine Lamb 171
Falafel. 173

About the Authors 174
A Note of Thanks 175
Photography End Notes 176
Photography Credits 177
About Sophia Institute 178

DEDICATION

No one is closer to the pope than the Swiss Guard.

Standing sentry at the gate at the Port Sant' Anna and the residence at the Apostolic Palace, flanking the altar during papal Mass or pacing the Popemobile as it rolls through St. Peter's Square, the Swiss Guard is always there, loyal and vigilant.

No one knows Vatican City better than the Swiss Guard.

From the museums to the Sistine Chapel, cobblestone streets to sprawling gardens, Apostolic Palace to the basilica, the Swiss Guard is stalwart protector of all.

It is only with the cooperation and assistance of the Swiss Guard that we are able to present this compilation of special recipes, stories, and imagery inspired by the Vatican and set in the glory and wonder of the Christmas season.

We hope that it brings some comfort and joy to all.

With gratitude and appreciation for their service to fifty popes and the Church of Rome for more than 500 years, we dedicate this book to the Pontifical Swiss Guard of the Holy See.

FOREWORD

I met Pope John Paul II for the first time the first Christmas Eve I served as a Swiss Guard. Having to work on that special night was not what I imagined life would be like for me in Rome and I struggled mightily that evening, even regretting that I signed up to serve the Holy Father. I shed more than one tear on my lonely assignment that night.

My post was immediately outside his apartment and, after his Christmas dinner, the pope used my exit to leave the apartment. As he greeted me, he noticed both that I was new and my red eyes. "Of course, this must be your first time away from home for Christmas!" This is how it happened that the first time I met the Holy Father as one of his bodyguards, I actually cried. The good pope embraced me, told me that he was very glad I was there, and that he would go and pray for me as he celebrated midnight Mass.

Since that night, in my life, Christmas has always been the glorious feast day deeply connected to John Paul II and my service in the Swiss Guard.

In this wonderful new book, my friend and colleague David Geisser reminisces about his time in the service of the successor of Saint Peter. He does it, of course, the way he knows best—through recipes that evoke life at the Vatican, service in the Guard, and the joy of Christmas. Combined with the compelling narratives of Christmas at the Vatican and around the world provided by Thomas Kelly, *The Vatican Christmas Cookbook* secures status as an ideal cookbook for what will surely be an extraordinary holiday season this year and for many years to come.

I hope you will enjoy these wonderful stories and both create and savor the food that they evoke, along with the fine art and imagery of the historic times and places of the Vatican.

Acriter et Fideliter (Fiercely and Faithfully),
Andreas Widmer
Swiss Guard Emeritus

Andreas Widmer served in the Swiss Guard under Pope John Paul II. He is a Swiss business executive, innovator, academic, and philanthropist. He is an assistant professor at the Catholic University of America and the author of the book The Pope and the CEO. *As Swiss Guard Emeritus, his continued service and representation of the principles of the Guard in Switzerland, Rome, and the United States has earned Andreas Widmer the unofficial title of "Swiss Guard Ambassador to America."*

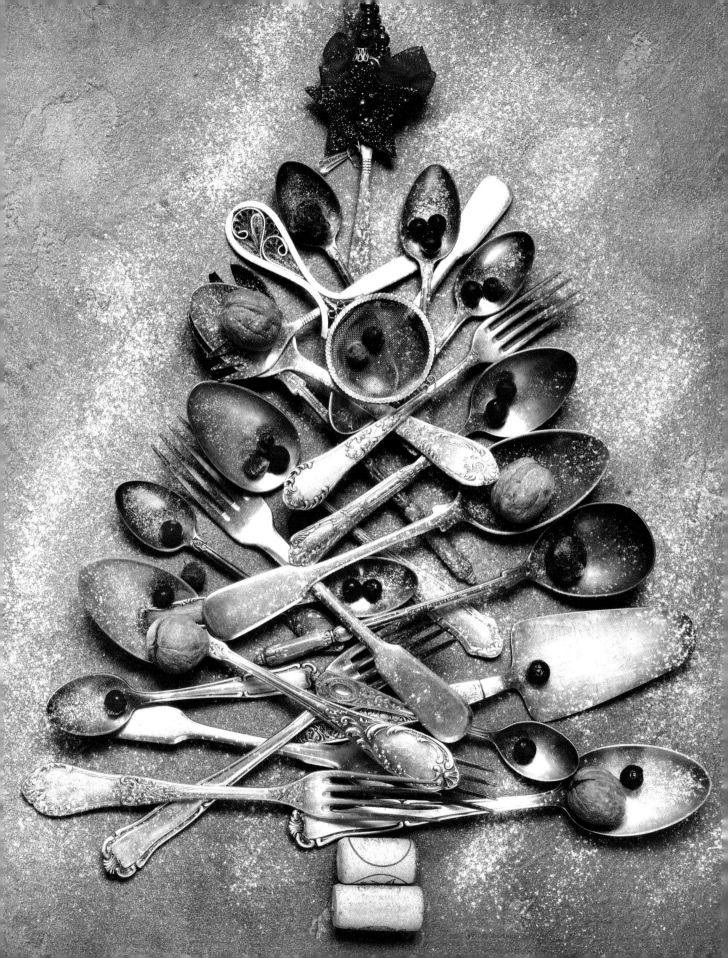

INTRODUCTION

In so many ways, the world is different than it was only a few short months ago, but there are some fundamentals that remain unchanged. One of them is food. Food is essential. Food is the sustenance of life. And food has been the focus of my life's work since I was a child.

When my friend, Thomas Kelly, proposed a Christmas sequel to *The Vatican Cookbook* that we collaborated with many others to create four years ago, I thought it was a wonderful idea. I was pleased with the process and the result of our work together. The collection of many new and classic recipes, surrounded by the splendor of the Vatican and enhanced by the stories of the Swiss Guard, was worthy of its title. I welcomed the opportunity to take that same concept and infuse it with the Christmas spirit and all the meaning and glory of that special season. It seemed a perfect fit to me.

There are elegant recipes here, gourmet food prepared and well-served in the haute cuisine manner. Any cookbook would do well to include exceptional innovations and stunning presentations that are feasts for the eyes.

There are many more recipes that are simple and satisfying. For most meals, ease of preparation is important, especially in difficult times or complicated circumstances, as are so prevalent today.

We have also included several communal meals, from fondues to fajitas, meant to be shared at table among friends, family, and guests. These are the best of meals because they encourage and emphasize the human touch. We gather close to each other, pass the vittles and plates from one to another, talk and laugh, enjoy the human moment with food as companion.

Enjoy.

David Geisser
Swiss Guard Emeritus

Advent

WAITING FOR THE COMING OF OUR LORD

Izaiáš   Jeremiáš   Ezechie

The roots of Advent run deep in the Messianic prophecies of the Old Testament, going all the way back to the books of Daniel, Ezekiel, Jeremiah, and Deuteronomy. Isaiah foretold: "For a child will be born to us, a son will be given to us; And the government will rest on His shoulders; And His name will be called Wonderful Counselor, Mighty God, Eternal Father, Prince of Peace" (9:6). Zechariah calls out, "Shout in triumph, O daughter of Jerusalem! Behold, your king is coming to you; He is just and endowed with salvation, humble, and mounted on a donkey" (9:9).

From ancient days, there was widespread belief in the coming of a Messiah, one who would bring deliverance and salvation for all. The people believed and waited, waited for hundreds of years for the coming of the Messiah.

For Christians, the four Sundays before Christmas came to be known as the time of waiting and preparation for the coming of the Lord. Observance of Advent began early in the fifth century with the practice of solemn prayer and fasting. Over the next hundred years, the Church formalized her practices for the season, officially setting the beginning of Advent on the Sunday nearest to the last day of November.

A homily of Saint Leo the Great constitutes the first papal declaration to discuss the season of Advent. In it, the pope urges Christians to fast, give to the poor, and act with humility as a way to "prepare themselves worthily to celebrate the anniversary of the Lord's coming into the world."

After Pope Leo's declaration, Advent customs and traditions began to evolve over many centuries and vary widely from place to place. One of the most enduring customs is the use of Advent candles, an arrangement of purple, pink, and white candles within a Christmas wreath. The candles are lit one at a time on consecutive Sundays and signify the aspirations and meaning of the season. The first stands for Hope, the second for Preparation, the third for Joy, and the fourth for Love. The last candle, placed in the center of the wreath, is the Christ candle, lit on Christmas morning.

Prepare ye the way of the Lord...
—ISAIAH 40:3

THE COMING OF THE GUARD
Advent 1505

There was turmoil across the European continent at the beginning of the sixteenth century, with the Italian Wars raging. Armies of the French, the Borgias, Habsburgs, Neapolitans, and the Holy Roman Empire vied for territory and treasure. At the center of it all was the Church of Rome, long dominant in religious affairs and moral authority, which inevitably had been caught up in the secular issues and conflicts of the day.

Soon after Cardinal Giuliano della Rovere was made Pope Julius II in 1503, he determined that the Vatican was in dire need of a military force for safety and protection. He reached out to his allies in the Swiss Confederacy and requested a permanent company of 200 of their finest fighting men to be stationed within the walls of Vatican City under the direct authority of the pope.

Swiss soldiers had been held in high esteem since ancient times. Roman historian Tacitus wrote that "The Helvetians [of central Switzerland] are a people of warriors, famous for the valor of their soldiers." No wonder that Pope Julius II chose to summon these "Swiss Guardians" to Rome during the troubled times.

In September of 1505, the Swiss soldiers departed on the arduous trek to Rome, led by Captain Kaspar von Silenen. They spent the Advent season crossing the Alps in the dead of winter, marched through northern Italy over the Christmas holiday, and arrived at the Vatican on January 22, 1506.

The group was inaugurated into the first class of the Pontifical Swiss Guard on that same day, with the personal blessing of Pope Julius II, and then welcomed into the barracks on the Via Pellegrino that had been constructed and prepared for them at the pope's direction.

Over more than 500 years since that day, the thousands of men who have served in the Pontifical Swiss Guard have never failed to "fiercely and faithfully" serve the Holy Father and defend the Holy See.

Advent

HEARTY BARLEY SOUP

Ingredients

1	Small leek
1	Carrot
1 stalk	Celery
2 ½ oz	Bündner dried beef (or substitute stew meat)
1	Onion
2	Bay leaves
2	Cloves
1 Tbsp	Butter
3 ½ oz	Pearl barley
6 cups	Beef bouillon
3 ½ Tbsp	Heavy cream
1 bunch	Chives
	Salt & pepper from the mill
1	Small veal shank or other soup bone (optional)

Preparation

Wash the leek and cut lengthwise into fine strips. Peel carrot and celery. Cut them both into cubes. Cut dried beef into cubes. Peel the onion, cut it in half, and stuff 1 bay leaf and 1 clove into each half onion.

Warm the butter in a large, deep frying pan. Add the leeks, carrot, celery, and dried beef, cover the pan, and cook on low for about 5 minutes. Add the barley, onion halves, bay leaf, and clove. Cover and cook for another minute or so. You may add a small soup bone for flavor, if you wish. A veal shank bone is a good choice.

Add the bouillon, bring to a boil, then reduce heat, and simmer over a low flame for about 2 hours, uncovered. Remove the onions, bay leaf, and clove, and the soup bone. Season to taste with salt and pepper.

If you wish to thicken the broth, stir in the heavy cream and cook briefly, just to warm it a bit, not even to simmer. Finely chop the chives, sprinkle over the soup, and add a sprig of dill or rosemary for garnish.

APPLE BREAD

Ingredients

3 ½ lbs	Apples
1 ⅔ cups	Dried figs
1 ⅔ cups	Dried plums
¾ cup	Dried apricots
¾ cup	Dates
⅔ cup	Plum liqueur
2 cups	Ground hazelnuts
1 ¾ cups	Sugar
6 cups	Flour
2 Tbsp	Baking powder
5 Tbsp	Ground Ceylon cinnamon
2 ½ Tbsp	Gingerbread spice
1 ½ Tbsp	Cocoa powder
½ Tbsp	Sea salt

Preparation

Quarter the apples and remove the core casings and seeds. Do not peel. Then grate the apples into a bowl, careful to retain juice.

Halve the figs, plums, apricots, and dates. Mix the grated apples and juice, dried fruit, and ground hazelnuts together and mix with the plum liqueur.

Set aside this mixture in a large bowl and let breathe for 2 hours. Then add the flour, baking powder, cinnamon, gingerbread spice, cocoa powder, sugar, and sea salt and mix all well.

Preheat oven to 350°. Form 2 equal-sized bread loaves and place them on a baking sheet covered with parchment paper and bake for about 50–55 minutes.

At first glance, Apple Bread would be called a fruitcake or some such hard and heavy pastry, regular gift at Christmas but never else. True Apple Bread is thick with dried fruit and spelt wheat, baked to perfection and served with butter melting. This is not a cake but the richest of breads, with crisp crust, rich with flavor and savory within. Apple Bread is a year-round treasure in Switzerland.

PUMPKIN SOUP AMARETTO

Ingredients

Yields about 12 cups

1½ lbs	Pumpkin (medium sized)
1	Onion
2 cups	Vegetable stock
½ cup	Heavy cream
2 Tbsp	Amaretto
1 Tbsp	Lavender honey
2 tsp	Ground ginger
2 tsp	Cardamom
	Olive oil for frying
	Salt & pepper from the mill

Preparation

Peel the onion and cut it into large cubes. Remove the seeds from the pumpkin with a spoon. Peel and halve the pumpkin, cutting it into large pieces. Braise the onion in a saucepan with oil until translucent. Then add the pumpkin and continue to braise for 10 minutes. Pour in the stock and let it boil until the pumpkin is tender.

Add the cream and bring to a boil. Puree the soup with a hand blender. Then add the spices, amaretto, and honey. Season with salt and pepper, if you wish. Ladle the soup into soup cups or, even better, hollowed-out small pumpkins. Serve hot.

SAINT NICHOLAS
December 6

Nicholas was born into a prestigious family in 270 AD in the coastal town of Patara in Asia Minor. Already known for their charitable endeavors, his parents died while leading efforts to help the sick during the Cyprian Plague.

Orphaned, and still young, Nicholas courageously took charge of his own affairs and proved wise beyond his years. He could have lived a life of ease, but he was determined to use his privileged position and inheritance to help the poor, sick, and needy.

There were so many anonymous acts of kindness that the local people realized that only Nicholas could be the secret benefactor. Lore tells of the plight of a poor family with three daughters, all without the means for a dowry. Without a dowry, the girls had dim marriage prospects, a single life of hard labor, or worse. Nicholas went to their home under cover of night and tossed gold coins through the open window. Some landed in the shoes or stockings left to dry by the fire.

Nicholas answered the call to a pious life and was ordained a priest. Soon after, despite his youth, he was named bishop of Myra in Lycia. His good acts and secret philanthropy continued on a larger scale.

There were tales of his benevolent exploits, from admirable to miraculous. He rescued a kidnapped child, saved three more from certain death, and calmed the seas for a foundering ship. He was loved and revered, but not by all. The Romans were wary of Nicholas for his influence and the rumors of his extraordinary powers. Imprisoned under Diocletian, then released by Constantine, he returned to his generous ways as an active bishop, benefactor, and "worker of wonders."

Widely recognized as a saint during his lifetime, Nicholas became St. Nicholas shortly after his death. He was one of the most popular saints of the first millennium, and he remains popular today as the beloved Santa Claus. The devotion to St. Nicholas, who was known as "Sinterklaas" in the Netherlands, traveled through Dutch immigrants who were among the first to celebrate Christmas in the New World, where the name developed into the "Santa Claus" that is known today.

Despite the name changes and the red-and-white suit, Santa Claus still serves as an immortalized remembrance of the overwhelming generosity and charity of St. Nicholas, the beloved early saint and wonder worker.

LITTLE SANTAS

Ingredients

4 cups	Bread flour
1 tsp	Sea salt
¼ cup	Sugar
¼ cup	Melted butter
¾ cup	Whole milk
½ cup	Low-fat quark butter (may substitute low-fat cream cheese)
1 ⅔ Tbsp	Yeast
1	Egg yolk
1 Tbsp	Whole milk for brushing
	Zest of 1 lemon
½ cup	Golden raisins for garnish

Preparation

Mix the flour, salt, and sugar in a large bowl. Crumble the yeast and dissolve in warm (not hot) milk. Stir briskly. Add the warm butter, quark, and warm milk to the flour mixture. Then add the zest of a lemon. Knead the mixture to a soft, smooth dough. Cover with a kitchen towel and leave at room temperature for at least 2 hours.

Preheat oven to 400°. Cut the dough mixture into eight equal sized pieces on a lightly floured work surface and then mold into Santa shapes, about the size of mini croissants. Decorate with raisins for eyes and mouth. Mix the egg yolks together with a tablespoon of milk. Brush the molded Little Santas with the egg yolk mass and then bake for about 20 minutes to a golden yellow. Depending on size and thickness, adjust the baking time: more for larger pieces, less for smaller. Monitor the baking and remove before the golden yellow turns to brown. Let them cool slightly before serving.

Little Santas are a new twist on Grittibänze, a centuries-old Swiss pastry typically served in the holiday season. Grittibänze means "bow-legged Benny" for the cartoonish character portrayed. Turning Benny into Santa is all in the art of shaping the dough. Santa is a bit fuller and rounded, with a full beard and tassled cap. Be as creative as you wish with the molding and enjoy.

Christmas Eve

"FOR UNTO US A CHILD
IS BORN, UNTO US
A SON IS GIVEN"

–ISAIAH 9:6

Christmas Eve

PAPALIN FETTUCCINE

Ingredients

1 lb	Fettuccine
8 oz	Raw ham, finely sliced
¾ cup	Green peas
1	Sweet onion
¾ cup	Pecorino, fresh grated
3	Egg yolks, whisked
⅔ cup	Heavy cream
1 ½ Tbsp	Olive oil
	Salt & pepper from the mill

Preparation

Boil the peas in salted water, drain, and set aside. Heat the olive oil in a frying pan. Peel the onion, cut into fine slices, and add to the frying pan. Fry the onions until glassy. Add the ham and fry to a light crisp. Add the boiled peas to the frying pan. Add the cream and simmer briefly. Season with sea salt and pepper. Cook the fettucine in plenty of salted water, drain, and add to the cream sauce. Remove the pan from the stove. Add the whisked egg yolks and pecorino and gently mix with the pasta and sauce.

Serve immediately.

Christmas Eve

PIZZA RACLETTE

Ingredients

Makes 20–25 single-serving pizzas

For the Dough

4 cups	White flour
2 Tbsp	Dry yeast
1 ¼ cups	Lukewarm water
1 ½ tsp	Salt
½ Tbsp	Olive oil
½ tsp	Oregano
	Olive oil for brushing

Pizza Toppings

Tomato sauce

Bacon

Ham

Minced sausage

Capers

Onions

Olives

Mushrooms

Artichoke hearts

Gorgonzola cheese, crumbled

Mozzarella cheese, shredded

Olive oil

Sea salt

Pepper, freshly ground

Preparation

Mix the white flour, oregano, and sea salt in a bowl. Dissolve the yeast in the lukewarm water. Pour the dissolved yeast and olive oil into the flour and knead until the dough no longer sticks to your hands. Cover the dough and set aside for 1 hour. Then, divide the dough into many pieces and shape them into balls with the palms. Make them about the size of limes, no larger. Every ball becomes a single serving. Let the dough balls rest for another 20 minutes.

In the meantime, cut the pizza topping ingredients into small pieces as necessary and place them in separate small bowls. Brush the raclette pans with a little olive oil and press the dough flat into the raclette molds. Spread tomato sauce liberally and top with the desired ingredients. Cover with mozzarella cheese and gorgonzola cheese accents. Insert into raclette and cook until cheeese is golden brown.

Christmas Eve

LASAGNA BOLOGNESE

Ingredients

1 lb	Lean ground beef
1	Onion, chopped
1 clove	Garlic, chopped
2 ribs	Celery
1	Carrot
2 Tbsp	Tomato paste
1 ¼ cups	Red wine
¾ cup	Beef bouillon
3 cups	Tomato sauce
1 Tbsp	Marjoram leaves
2 Tbsp	Butter, for the pan
12 oz	Lasagna pasta, cooked
¾ cup	Parmesan cheese, grated
	Olive oil for frying
	Salt & pepper from the mill

For the Béchamel Sauce

3 Tbsp	Butter
¼ cup	White flour
2 cups	Whole milk
	Nutmeg
	Salt & pepper from the mill

Preparation

Sauté the onions and garlic briefly in the olive oil. Then add the ground meat and fry on a high heat. Meanwhile, wash and peel the celery and carrot, and cut into small pieces. Add the vegetables and the tomato paste to the pan, stir in thoroughly, and pour in the red wine. Bring the red wine to a boil for about 5 minutes, then add the bouillon, tomato sauce, and marjoram leaves, and simmer gently for about 1 hour at a very low heat.

Meanwhile, for the béchamel sauce, melt the butter in a saucepan, add the flour and stir with a cooking spoon for half a minute. Add the milk and bring to a boil with the help of a hand mixer, stirring constantly, until the sauce is thick and creamy. Season the béchamel sauce to taste with sea salt, nutmeg, and pepper.

Preheat the oven to 400°. Butter a large, rectangular gratin pan and start with a layer of Bolognese sauce, then add a layer of lasagna sheets. Cover lasagna with a layer of Bolognese sauce, béchamel sauce, and a little grated cheese. Repeat this process until the pan is full. The top layer should consist of béchamel sauce sprinkled with grated cheese. Bake for about 40 minutes on the low rack of the oven until the top appears crispy. Serve right at the table, cutting generous portions from the gratin pan.

Christmas Eve

POLISH BORSCHT

Ingredients

10 oz	Red beet (2 medium beets), cubed
1	Onion, chopped
1	Small leek, sliced
2 Tbsp	Butter
2 ½ cups	Vegetable bouillon
4 Tbsp	Red wine
¾ cup	Heavy cream
	Salt & pepper from the mill

Preparation

Peel the beets and cut into cubes. Wash the leek and cut it into thin strips. Peel and chop the onion. Heat the butter in a deep frying pan and add the chopped vegetables. Add the red wine and vegetable bouillon and simmer for about 40 minutes. Then puree everything finely in a blender and brush through a fine sieve. Simmer the soup again over a low heat for 15 minutes. Meanwhile, beat the heavy cream to a thick texture and fold into the soup. Season with sea salt and pepper. Pour into shallow bowls or glassware and serve with colorful garnish.

Although known as Borscht in the Ukraine and Russia, Barszcz is a red beet root soup that is a staple of Polish cuisine and always a part of the traditional Christmas Eve family supper. All the sour beet soups have an ancient heritage, dating back to the days when Slavic tribes foraged for wild herbs and root vegetables to make soups and stews. There are countless variations of Borscht, from a simple, clear broth to a thick and rich meal.

Christmas

THE NATIVITY OF OUR LORD

aint Luke the Evangelist delivers the most joyful story of the Gospel, told in the manner of a first-hand news account, with respect for the facts and awe at the extraordinary events that transpired on that most holy night. It is worthy of reading aloud again and again every Christmas.

GOSPEL OF LUKE
CHAPTER 2, VERSES 1–19

Now it happened that at this time Caesar Augustus issued a decree that a census should be made of the whole inhabited world. This census—the first—took place while Quirinius was governor of Syria, and everyone went to be registered, each to his own town.

So Joseph set out from the town of Nazareth in Galilee for Judaea, to David's town called Bethlehem, since he was of David's House and line, in order to be registered together with Mary, his betrothed, who was with child.

Now it happened that, while they were there, the time came for her to have her child, and she gave birth to a son, her first-born. She wrapped him in swaddling clothes and laid him in a manger because there was no room for them in the inn.

In the countryside close by there were shepherds out in the fields keeping guard over their sheep during the watches of the night.

An angel of the Lord stood over them and the glory of the Lord shone round them. They were terrified, but the angel said, "Do not be afraid. Look, I bring you news of great joy, a joy to be shared by the whole people. Today in the town of David, a Savior has been born to you. He is Christ the Lord. And here is a sign for you: you will find a baby wrapped in swaddling clothes and lying in a manger."

And all at once with the angel there was a great throng of the hosts of heaven, praising God with the words:

> Glory to God in the high-
> est heaven, and on earth
> peace for those he favors.

Now it happened that when the angels had gone from them into heaven, the shepherds said to one another, "Let us go to Bethlehem and see this event which the Lord has made known to us."

So they hurried away and found Mary and Joseph, and the baby lying in the manger.

When they saw the child they repeated what they had been told about him, and everyone who heard it was astonished at what the shepherds said to them.

As for Mary, she treasured all these things and pondered them in her heart.

STUFFED CHICKEN BREAST WITH PEPPERS

Ingredients

4	Chicken breasts
1	Red pepper
1	Yellow pepper
1	Small savoy cabbage
	Olive oil for frying
	Salt & pepper from the mill
4	Toothpicks

Mashed Sweet Potatoes

3 lbs	Sweet potatoes
⅔ cup	Butter
⅔ cup	Milk
⅔ cup	Heavy cream
1 ¼ cups	Grated Parmesan
	Ground nutmeg
	Salt & pepper from the mill

For the Sauce

4 oz	Amontillado sherry
4	Egg yolks
4	Star anise
½	Vanilla pod
	Sea salt

Preparation

Wash the meat and pat dry. Wash the vegetables as well. Cut the chicken breasts on the side so that they can be opened and filled. Blanch 4 large leaves of the savoy cabbage in salt water for a few minutes, immediately quench them cold and cut out the stalk. Cut out the core casing of the peppers and cut 4 strips about ½ inch wide and 2 ½ inches long from each type of pepper. Then place one stick of each pepper on the cabbage leaf, roll it into a roulade and stuff carefully into chicken breasts. Reseal the meat with the toothpick. Now sear the meat on all sides in a frying pan and then place in the oven preheated to 350° until a core temperature of 150° is reached, about 45–55 minutes.

Peel the sweet potatoes and cut them into cubes. Then cook the potatoes softly in boiling salted water. Pour soft potatoes into a sieve and let them evaporate briefly. In the meantime, bring the butter, milk, and cream to a boil in a pot, then add the cooked potato pieces. Make a fine puree from the potatoes with a potato masher or food processor. Finally, season the puree with parmesan, salt, and nutmeg.

Put the star anise together with the sherry in a small pot, bring to a boil and immediately set aside to cool. Beat the egg yolks until they are foamy in a metal bowl, then slowly pour in the cooled sherry and whisk over a double boiler to a foamy light cream. Carefully scrape out the pulp of the vanilla pod and add to the mixture. Finally, season with sea salt.

Slice each stuffed chicken breast in thick sections and place atop a bed of sweet potato puree on individual plates. Spoon the star anise sauce over all, and serve.

VEAL TARTARE IN TRUFFLE OIL

Ingredients

½ lb	Veal tartare
1	Egg yolk
1 tsp	Dijon mustard
2 tsp	Truffle oil
2 tsp	Olive oil
½	Shallot
½ bunch	Chives
	Salt & pepper from the mill

For the Blinis

½ cup	White flour
½ cup	Buckwheat flour
2 tsp	Fresh yeast
⅔ cup	Whole milk
3 Tbsp	Butter
1	Egg white
	Olive oil for frying
½ tsp	Sea salt

Preparation

Finely chop the shallot and chives. In a large bowl, whisk the egg yolk and the mustard together. Drizzle the truffle oil and olive oil slowly into the mixture, whisking briskly until emulsified. Then add the meat, the chopped shallot, ¾ of the chopped chives, and mix with a fork to a homogeneous mass. Season with salt and pepper.

Warm the milk to lukewarm and add the yeast, stirring well. Melt the butter in a small saucepan. Combine the buckwheat flour, white flour, and salt in a large bowl and form a hollow in the middle. Pour the milk with the dissolved yeast and butter into the bowl and work the whole into a smooth dough.

Cover and let the dough rise for about 2 hours. Then beat the egg whites until stiff and fold carefully into the dough. Set a frying pan over medium heat and drizzle with olive oil. Fry the dough in blinis ½ tablespoon in size, making them as round as possible using a spoon. Fry the blinis for about 1 minute, until golden on the underside, then flip and cook the other side for about a ½ minute.

Serve the blinis topped with the tartare and garnish with the remaining chopped chives. Makes about 24 pieces.

FILET MIGNON WITH RACY PEPPER SAUCE

Ingredients

2 lbs	Beef filets (4 filets, 8 oz each)
1 sprig	Thyme, large
1 clove	Garlic
	Olive oil for frying
	Salt & pepper from the mill

For the Pepper Sauce

¼ cup	Pickled green peppercorns
2	Shallots
½ cup	Brandy
1 cup	Beef bouillon
¾ cup	Cream
½ Tbsp	Sea salt
½ tsp	Corn starch, if necessary
	Olive oil for frying

Preparation

Preheat the oven to 175°. Rub the filets vigorously with salt and pepper on all sides.

Fry in a pan with a little oil at medium-high heat for 3–5 minutes, then flip and fry for 3–5 minutes more. Add the thyme and garlic clove and cook in the oven to a core temperature of 125°. This should take about 30 minutes, but time can vary widely for size and thickness of fillets. Use a meat thermometer to confirm.

For the pepper sauce, peel and finely chop the shallots. Drain the peppercorns. Now put the dry peppercorns in a hot saucepan, add the shallot cubes and the brandy. Reduce the liquid until it is almost gone, then stir in the bouillon. Let this brew simmer slightly for about 20 minutes, then pass the brew through a sieve, and let the liquid boil to reduce by ⅓. (Be sure to save the peppercorns from the sieve and set aside.) Add the cream and bring to a gentle boil. If necessary, bind the sauce with ½ teaspoon of corn starch dissolved in water. Salt to taste, then add the peppercorns and cubed shallots back into the sauce.

To finish, set each filet mignon on a single serving plate, surrounded by the pepper sauce and decorated with the peppercorns and thyme.

My favorite presentation for this recipe is to place the filet mignon on a hefty serving of Red Beet Risotto (see this recipe in the "Dishes on the Side" section), enough to frame the filet, surrounding it with its luscious color. It makes for a striking visual at the moment the dish is served and is even more pleasing to the palate, as the juices from the filet mingle with the velvet texture of the risotto.

THE HISTORY
of Christmas

Christmas, or "Christ's Mass," was not always the widely-celebrated social and religious holiday that it is known as today. For more than three hundred years after Christ was born, there was no Christmas, no Christmas Mass, no celebration. The date of our Lord's birth was unknown; records nonexistent. It wasn't until the fourth century that the Church initiated an exhaustive search into the facts of the life of Christ. After review of historical records and consultation among the Church hierarchy, Pope Julius I proclaimed the date of the birth of Christ as December 25, and so it remains to this day.

Coincident or not, there were seasonal festivities across many cultures at the time of the winter solstice—the Yule in Nordic and Celtic lands, the festival of Odin in the German regions, and the Saturnalia in Rome. Most of these were raucous pagan fests to which Christians responded with the holy rites of Christmas.

Christmas was slow to take hold in the New World. First arrivals from Christian Europe were the Puritans in 1620, a stern Protestant sect, dismissive of holidays or celebrations of any kind. For decades, Christmas was banned in Boston.

It was well into the nineteenth century before Christmas emerged as a prominent holiday, spurred by waves of immigrants from their Christmas-loving homelands in Europe and endorsed by widely popular stories like Charles Dickens' *A Christmas Carol*. Christmas officially was declared a national holiday in the United States in 1870. Americans embraced Christmas and reimagined the celebration, adopting and adapting the best of the myriad customs and traditions: family gatherings, charity and gift-giving, Christmas trees and Christmas carols, mistletoe and egg nog, and Santa Claus, of course.

Christmas is a time of charity, with more charitable acts and donations made than any other time of year. Christmas is a time of love, celebrating the bonds of family and friends and kindness to strangers. Christmas is a time of joy, as the fundamental meaning and spirit of the day has remained unchanged since that morning in Bethlehem so long ago.

PORK TENDERLOIN IN PUFF PASTRY

Ingredients

1½ lbs	Pork tenderloin
2 oz	Coppacola ham, thinly sliced
½ lb	Veal sausage meat
1	Puff pastry, sized to the roast
1	Mozzarella log (6 oz)
12	Green olives, pitted
6 strips	Sun-dried tomatoes
1 Tbsp	Capers
1	Egg yolk
	Olive oil for frying
	Salt & pepper from the mill

Preparation

Finely chop the capers, olives, and dried tomatoes. Cut the mozzarella in thin slices. Season the pork fillet with salt and pepper and fry in a frying pan with oil to sear.

Preheat oven to 350°. Cut the meat lengthwise. Fill with mozzarella and the chopped olives, capers, and tomatoes. Roll out the puff pastry and sprinkle with sausage. Spread the coppacola slices on the roast and place the filled pork fillet on the edge of the dough. Now gently roll the fillet into the dough. Place the whole thing on a baking sheet lined with parchment paper, brush with the egg yolk, and bake for about 30–40 minutes. Use a meat thermometer to confirm temperature of pork reaches 160°.

Let rest briefly, then cut the warm pastry-encrusted tenderloin into thick slabs and serve on a large cutting board. Distribute to individual plates at the table.

Christmas

LAMB WITH HERB CRUST & MEDITERRANEAN VEGETABLES

Ingredients

4 pieces	Lamb rump (6 oz each)
3 Tbsp	Butter
1	Small shallot
1 clove	Garlic
3 slices	Hard toasted bread
½ cup	Parmesan, grated
1 bunch	Flat-leaf parsley
1 sprig	Fresh thyme
	Olive oil for frying
	Salt & pepper from the mill

Mediterranean Vegetables

2 ½ lbs	Small potatoes
1	Yellow pepper
1	Red pepper
1	Zucchini
1	Small eggplant
7 oz	Cherry tomatoes
1 sprig	Rosemary
1 sprig	Thyme
	Lemon oil to drizzle
	Olive oil for frying
	Sea salt

Preparation

Finely chop the shallot and garlic, and the parsley and thyme. Cut the crusts from the toast slices and reduce toast to very fine crumbs with food processor. Add the chopped shallot and garlic to buttered pan over a medium heat. Add the chopped toast and the chopped herbs to the pan and mix. Allow to cool a bit, then mix in the parmesan and season with salt and pepper. Wash the meat, pat dry, and season with salt and pepper. Heat the olive oil in a separate saucepan. Add the meat and fry well over high heat on both sides for about 5 minutes. Preheat oven to 175°.

In the meantime, quarter the potatoes and pluck the rosemary and thyme. Then fry the potatoes in a frying pan with oil, turning often, for about 25–30 minutes, until crispy. Add the rosemary and thyme to the pan for the last 5 minutes. Season with sea salt.

While potatoes are frying, move the meat from the pan to the oven for at least 30 minutes, until cooked through. Remove and increase oven heat to 450°. Spread the herb crust evenly on the pieces of meat and press well. Put the meat on the top rack in the oven and let the crust bake over for 3–5 minutes.

Halve the peppers, remove the core casing, and cut the peppers into small cubes. Cut the zucchini and eggplant into small cubes. Halve the cherry tomatoes, remove the seeds, and cut into small cubes. Heat all the vegetables (except tomatoes) briefly with oil in a separate pan, careful to preserve the crunch. Add the tomatoes just before the end of the cooking time. Season with sea salt and drizzle some lemon oil over the vegetables.

To serve, place lamb steaks on individual plates, cover with the vegetable mix and garnish with the fried potatoes.

VENISON IN FIG SAUCE

Ingredients

1 lb	Roe deer tenderloins
2½ cups	Figs
¾ cup	Port wine
½ cup	Red wine
¾ cup	Wildfond (or organic vegetable stock)
¼ cup	Heavy cream
1	Cinnamon stick
2	Cloves
1 tsp	Corn starch
	Salt & pepper from the mill
	Green sprouts for garnish

Preparation

Preheat oven to 175°. Wash the meat and pat dry. Season with salt and pepper and fry on both sides in a frying pan. Cook the deer tenderloins in the oven until they reach a core temperature of 140°.

Wash the figs. Pour the port wine and red wine into a small pot, add all the figs at once and simmer softly over a low heat with the lid on.

Then crush the soft figs with a fork and pass the sauce through a fine sieve, straining it into a small pot. Place the pot on the stove and let the sauce simmer until it becomes syrupy. Place the lid loosely on the pan and reduce the liquid by about half, then add the cream and simmer again for a minute or so. Stir in a teaspoon of corn starch mixed with cold water and continue cooking to bring the sauce to the desired consistency.

To serve, cut the fillets into large pieces, arrange on the plates, drizzle the sauce over them, and garnish with the sprouts.

Christmas

TAGLIATELLE PORCINI

Ingredients

14 oz	Tagliatelle pasta
14 oz	Porcini mushrooms
2	Shallots
⅓ cup	Flat-leaf parsley
1 ½ Tbsp	Olive oil
3 ½ Tbsp	Butter
1 cup	Heavy cream
½ cup	Parmesan cheese, grated
¼ cup	Gorgonzola cheese, mild
	Salt & pepper from the mill

Preparation

Clean the mushrooms and cut them into slices. Peel and finely chop the shallots. Wash the parsley, dry, pluck from the stems, and finely chop. Heat the olive oil in a frying pan, add the shallots and cook to glassy, then add the porcini mushrooms and sauté briefly. Remove from the heat, add the parsley, and season to taste with sea salt and pepper.

Cook the tagliatelle to *al dente* in plenty of salted water and drain. Melt the butter in a saucepan, add the cooked pasta and parmesan. Mix well, add the cream, and mix again. Season with sea salt and pepper and arrange on plates. Spread out the porcini mushrooms over the pasta on the plates, and finish with crumbles of gorgonzola over all.

CHRISTMAS
at the Vatican

Roman Christmas markets showcase jewel-like candies and delicate olive wood ornaments, while resounding the joyful greetings: *Buon Natale!* and *Felice anno nuovo!* Twinkling lights web through every street and the scents of roasting chestnuts and *cioccolato caldo* fill the air. After the obligatory slice of *panettone*, often enjoyed with a bubbling glass of Prosecco, one inevitably is drawn through the streets into the arms of St. Peter's piazza. Hidden behind barriers at the piazza's center, a towering tree slowly amasses decorations and a life-sized *presepio* starts to take shape. Excitement only grows as passersby catch glimpses of the hidden décor.

All excitedly await the unveiling of the *presepio*, a detailed Nativity scene, which is said to have been first used by St. Francis of Assisi to tell the age-old story of the little Son born of a Virgin. Every church in the city, along with homes, cafes, and offices, proudly display these meticulously detailed Nativity scenes. The unveiling of the *presepio* in St. Peter's Square, a long-awaited event, culminates with the lighting of the massive tree. The scene draws crowds together from around the world in prayer and celebration. Traditional Italian bagpipers, or *zampognari*,

dress as shepherds and play reverently for the Christ Child. At other times, ethereal choirs sing alongside the scene of Bethlehem. Each year, visitors to the piazza tell the Nativity story to their children and grandchildren in every language.

Advent draws to an end with the celebration of the Christmas Eve Vigil Mass, for which thousands file into St. Peter's Basilica. At the end of the Mass, the choir triumphantly sings *Adeste Fideles*, and the pope processes with a figure of the Infant to a side chapel near the entrance of the basilica. There, he gently places the Babe in a *presepio*. The Church unites in its celebrations as parishes in Rome and throughout the world participate in similar processions.

The pope then gives his Urbi et Orbi blessing to the world. At the end of the Christmas liturgies, crowds flow from St. Peter's, the very heart of the Church, carrying the blessings and hope of new birth. Joy runs through the veins of the Eternal City with the promise of food, merriment, and copious amounts of *panettone*.

Buon Natale!
Hannah O'Connor
Rome Program Residence Director,
Thomas More College of Liberal Arts

Christmas

MUGGI'S MINCEMEAT

Ingredients

½ lb	Beef minced meat
½ lb	Veal minced meat
½ lb	Pork minced meat
½ lb	Veal sausage
1	Onion
4 Tbsp	Parsley, finely chopped
1 cup	Breadcrumbs
1	Egg
4 Tbsp	Dry mustard
2 Tbsp	Worcestershire sauce
3 tsp	Tabasco sauce
	Salt & pepper from the mill
1	Carrot
1 stalk	Celery

For the Sauce

1	Carrot
1 stalk	Celery
1 tsp	Tomato puree
¾ cup	Red wine
3 cups	Vegetable bouillon (or vegetable broth)
	Olive oil for frying
3 Tbsp	Pommery mustard, coarse

Preparation

For the meat patties, peel and finely chop the onion. Sautè the onion in 1 tablespoon of olive oil until fragrant, about 2 minutes. Set aside to cool. Finely chop the parsley, carrot, and celery and add to the onions.

Mix all the minced meat and sausage into the onion mixture along with the bread crumbs, egg, mustard, fine chopped celery and carrots, and spices. Form this mixture into small, thick patties, about 3 oz in size. Sear the meat patties on both sides in a large saucepan with oil, remove, and set aside.

Add the onion mixture to the same pan, along with the tomato puree, and cook for several minutes. Add the wine and simmer on medium-high heat until the liquid reduces by half, then add the vegetable broth.

Return the patties to the pan and cook in the sauce for about half an hour or until meat is cooked through. Once cooked, remove the patties and pass the sauce through a sieve. Reduce the sauce to the desired consistency and gently whisk in the Pommery mustard, little by little. Let it swirl in the dark sauce. Serve patties set in a nest of potato puree (see Dishes on the Side) and smothered in the sauce.

ROASTED TROUT WITH FENNEL AND BAGUETTE

Ingredients

4	Trout fillets
1	Large fennel
2	Blood oranges
1	Large fresh baguette
2 cloves	Garlic
½ cup	Fennel seeds
½ cup	Crema di Balsamico
	Olive oil for frying
	Salt & pepper from the mill

Preparation

Peel the garlic and slice the baguette. Peel and quarter the blood oranges, then halve the quarters for eight thick slices each. Cut the fennel into thin strips. In a frying pan, heat the oil lightly and add the fennel until it has taken on a caramel color. Set aside, add the orange slices, and mix gently. Season with sea salt and pepper.

Roughly crush the fennel seeds with pestle and mortar. Salt the trout fillets and fry briefly on the skin side in a frying pan with oil. Then flip the fillets, reduce the heat, continue frying briefly until trout flakes easily with a fork, remove fillets, and set aside. In the same pan, rub the bottom with the garlic cloves and then fry the baguette slices to a golden yellow, adding a little more oil, if you wish.

Place each trout fillet atop a slice of baguette on separate plates, spread the fennel mixture over them. Decorate the plates with the crushed fennel seeds, splash a little Crema di Balsamico over all, serve and enjoy.

Christmas
VEAL CHANTERELLE

Ingredients

1 lb	Fillet of veal
¾ lb	Chanterelle mushrooms
1	Sweet onion, diced
½ cup	Dry white wine
1 cup	Heavy cream
¼ cup	Vegetable bouillon
1½ Tbsp	Ghee butter
2 pinches	Nutmeg, ground
1 bunch	Fresh mint
1 Tbsp	Fennel seeds, ground
½ tsp	Cumin
	Salt & pepper from the mill

Preparation

Carefully clean the mushrooms. Preheat oven to 160°. Peel and finely chop the onion and leave to simmer briefly in half a tablespoon of ghee. Add the mushrooms and sauté briefly, about 2 minutes. Wash the veal fillet, pat dry, and cut into thin slices. Then season the veal fillet with salt, pepper, fennel seeds, and cumin and sear in ghee on a high heat. Remove from the pan and warm in the oven. Drench the frying pan with white wine and reduce to four tablespoons. Add the heavy cream and vegetable bouillon and bring to boil. Add a pinch or two of nutmeg. Remove the meat from the oven and sear again briefly in the frying pan with the sauce. Garnish with fresh mint leaves.

Christmas

BEEF RIB MEDITERRANEAN

Ingredients

4	Large beef rib steaks (8 oz each)
2¼ lbs	Yukon Gold small potatoes
1	Yellow pepper
1	Red pepper
1	Zucchini
1	Eggplant
10	Black olives, pitted
10	Green olives, pitted
1 Tbsp	Capers
8	Sun-dried tomato strips in olive oil (from the jar)
1 sprig	Rosemary
1 sprig	Thyme
	Olive oil for cooking
	Salt & pepper from the mill
	Fleur de sel or fine sea salt

Preparation

Preheat the oven to 375°. Wash the vegetables and halve the potatoes. Halve the peppers, remove the core casings and white skins, then cut into coarse cubes. Cut the zucchini and eggplant into coarse cubes. Put all the vegetables and potatoes on a baking sheet and add the olives, dried tomatoes, and capers. Pluck the rosemary and thyme leaves from the stems and add to the vegetables. Now marinate all well with olive oil and season with sea salt. Place the baking sheet in the oven for about 40 minutes, until the potato-vegetable mixture is cooked through.

Meanwhile, season the beef with salt and pepper and fry in a large pan with oil. Then place in the oven, preheated to 175°, until the meat reaches a core temperature of 125° (medium rare). Serve along with the potatoes and vegetables and sprinkle with fleur de sel.

> *Fleur de sel is named for the flowery patterns of salt that form a thin, delicate crust on the surface of seawater as it evaporates. It has been prized since ancient times for its subtle flavor, the finest finishing salt for all dishes. Today, fleur de sel must be harvested by hand, with methods and tools that date back more than a thousand years. And still today, only young women are enlisted as paludierres to reap the fragile webs of tiny crystals from the shallow waters, as the most delicate touch is required.*

Christmas

CAPONATA GAMBERONI

Ingredients

For the Caponata

1	Small eggplant
2 stalks	Celery
1	Red pepper
1	Yellow pepper
2	Vine-ripe tomatoes
2	Small shallots
½ cup	Olive oil
½ tsp	Sugar
3½ oz	White wine vinegar
50	Pine nuts
50	Capers

For the Gamberoni

8	Giant prawns
1 sprig	Thyme
1 clove	Garlic
	Salt & pepper from the mill

For the Honey Marinade

⅓ cup	Honey
¼ cup	Soy sauce
2 tsp	Olive oil
1 tsp	Lemon juice
1 Tbsp	Fresh minced garlic
1 Tbsp	Chopped scallions
1 tsp	Fresh minced ginger

Caponata Preparation

Wash the vegetables thoroughly. Chop all vegetables into small cubes.

Bring water to a boil. Blanch the tomatoes for 10 seconds, quench in ice water, then peel.

Roast the pine nuts in a pan without fat.

Sauté the shallots in hot olive oil. Add the tomato cubes, sprinkle with sugar, and deglaze with vinegar. Set aside.

Fry the remaining vegetables in a second pan, add the shallot and tomato mixture, and refine with capers and pine nuts. Season with salt and pepper.

Add half of the honey marinade to the caponata and mix gently.

Gamberoni Preparation

Peel the giant prawns and remove the veins. Now fry in a hot pan for a few minutes. Add the sprigs of thyme and the clove of garlic shortly before the end of the cooking. Season with salt and pepper.

Honey Marinade Preparation

Whisk the honey, soy sauce, olive oil, lemon juice, garlic, scallions, and ginger all together in a medium bowl. Set aside to add before serving.

Serve on individual plates with one gamberoni placed atop the caponata, with the rest of the honey marinade drizzled over for best presentation.

SWISS GUARD
Christmas Watch

Christmas Eve and Christmas Day are the busiest and most demanding days of the year for the Swiss Guard. There are more activities and events on the calendar, both formal and impromptu, than any other month of the year.

Visitors from all over the world flock to Vatican City for a once-in-a-lifetime Christmas experience. From St. Peter's Square to the basilica, the museums to the Apostolic Palace, the Plaza Santa Maria to the Pigna Courtyard, there are people everywhere, all under the watchful eye of the Swiss Guard.

Pope Francis leads Midnight Mass on Christmas Eve and the solemn High Mass on Christmas Day, while making time for countless other events and appearances in Vatican City. These appearances beyond the gates most often involve His Holiness bringing Christmas cheer to the troubled and infirm. He may visit with children at an orphanage, elderly patients at a hospital, inmates at a prison. Through all the visits and celebrations, the Swiss Guard faithfully accompanies the Holy Father.

For most in the Guard, there is hardly a moment to rest. But there is respite for a fortunate few after the Midnight Mass. While a full complement of men remains on duty through the night, those that are relieved of duty until dawn the following day gather with their families for a late meal and brief celebration. There in the Swiss Guard dining hall, the families give out small gifts and candies to their children, sing carols, tell stories, toast the holiday, and end by praying together. It may seem modest, but these close Christmas Eve celebrations make for treasured memories in the minds of many Swiss Guard families.

Christmas

ROAST CHRISTMAS TURKEY

Ingredients

1	Fresh turkey (about 20 lbs)
½ cup	Butter, softened
1 tsp	Minced garlic
2 Tbsp	Sage leaves
2 Tbsp	Thyme leaves, chopped
¼ cup	Flat-leaf parsley, chopped
1 cup	Onions, chopped
1 cup	Celery, chopped
1 Tbsp	Olive oil for cooking
3 ⅓ cups	Coarse dried bread crumbs
2 cups	Water
1 cup	Assorted herbs, fresh from sprigs (choose from parsley, basil, thyme, sage)
3 cups	Chicken broth
	Blueberries & oranges for garnish

Preparation

Preheat the oven to 450°. Rinse turkey, inside and out, pat dry, and set aside for 20 minutes. Meanwhile, blend the butter, garlic, and herbs in a food processor until smooth.

Season the cavity of the turkey with salt and pepper. Sauté the chopped onions and celery briefly in olive oil. Place the bread crumbs in mixing bowl, moisten thoroughly with water, then add the onions, celery, and assorted herbs (parsley, sage, rosemary, and thyme), and mix well. Stuff the turkey with the bread crumb mix, full but not tight. Bind the turkey legs with twine.

Rub the herb butter on all exposed turkey skin. Keep the chicken broth warm in a saucepan on the stove over low heat. Insert meat thermometer deep into the turkey breast. Place turkey in a roasting pan, and roast in oven for 1 hour. Reduce temperature to 350° and continue roasting, basting with the chicken broth every 20 minutes or so, until meat thermometer reads 165° (about 4 ½ hours).

In the last hour or so of cooking, if the turkey is browning, remove from the oven and tent loosely with foil and return to the oven. When cooking is complete, set the turkey on display for 20 minutes as it cools to serving temperature. Return to kitchen to slice and separate, arrange on a large platter, and serve.

EGG WILLIAMS SOUFFLÉ

Ingredients

4	Large eggs
8 tsp	Crème fraiche
2 tsp	Williams brandy
	Butter for brushing
	Sea salt
	Salt & pepper from the mill

NOTE: Crème fraiche and Williams brandy are both worth the extra effort, but you may substitute sour cream for the crème and a good quality cognac for the brandy.

Preparation

Preheat the oven to 390°. Crack the eggs, place in a bowl, and mix with a whisk. Add the crème and Williams brandy and mix everything well. Season to taste with sea salt and freshly ground pepper.

Brush four glass, melamine, or porcelain ramekins (½ cup size) with butter. Gently fill the ramekins with the mixture to past halfway and then place in the oven for 10–15 minutes, until the egg concoction rises nicely.

Serve immediately.

POIRE WILLIAMS

The "Williams" in Egg Williams Soufflé is for Poire Williams, a very special eau de vie, a light, clear brandy made from the Williams pear (also known as Williams's bon chrétien in Europe and the Bartlett pear in the United States) through fermentation and double distillation.

A unique feature of Poire Williams is the bottling process by a few of the elite producers. They meticulously attach empty bottles to select buds on the branches of pear trees so that each pear grows to maturity inside the bottle, resulting in a stunning presentation.

Christmas

RICOTTA LEMON RAVIOLI

Ingredients

½ cup	Ricotta cheese
¾ cup	Parmesan cheese, grated
3	Egg yolks
	Zest of 1 lemon
4	Sage leaves
3½ oz	Fresh butter
2 oz	Parmesan, freshly shaved
	Salt & pepper from the mill

Preparation

Combine the ricotta, parmesan, egg yolks, and lemon zest and mix thoroughly. Set aside for ravioli filling.

Use ready-made, thin lasagna pasta sheets for ravioli pasta. Set out a pasta sheet and cut horizontal and vertical seams in 2-inch increments. Place teaspoonfuls of the cheese-egg mixture on the pasta sheet 2 inches apart, arranged in neat rows. Brush the seams of the pasta with cold water, then cover with a second sheet and press down firmly so that all the air escapes. Now cut through the pasta sheets along the seams with a knife or cookie cutter. Separate into individual raviolis and pinch gently around all the edges to seal.

Boil the little ravioli in water for about 3–5 minutes, then remove and set aside to drain. In the meantime, froth the butter with the sage leaves in a pan and pour over the ravioli. Serve promptly with freshly shaven parmesan sprinkled over for garnish.

Christmas

SALMON CLUB SANDWICH

Ingredients

For the Bread

4 cups	Bread flour (85% all-purpose, 15% spelt)
1 ½ tsp	Salt
2 Tbsp	Sugar
1 ⅔ Tbsp	Cube yeast, crushed
½ cup	Hard butter, cut in pieces
1 ¼ cups	Whole milk
1	Large Egg
1 Tbsp	Cream

For the Filling

⅓ cup	Mayonnaise
¼ cup	Dijon mustard
¾ Tbsp	Liquid honey
⅓ cup	Dill weed buds, finely chopped
	Sea salt
1 ⅓ lbs	Smoked salmon fillet
1	Apple
¼ cup	Alfalfa sprouts

Bread Preparation

Mix the flour, salt, and sugar in a bowl. Mix the crushed yeast in well. Add the butter and the milk, mix all, and knead to a soft, smooth dough. Cover the dough and set aside at room temperature for 90 minutes. Meanwhile, preheat the oven to 350°. Put the egg in a small cup, add the cream, and whisk with a fork. Then, when it is time, place the dough on a lightly floured work surface. Divide the dough into 3 equal portions, press to flatten slightly, then form together into long strands (28 inches), which are thicker in the middle and tapered at the ends. Weave strands together into a braid. Brush the braids with the egg mass and leave to rest for 30 minutes. Then bake the braids for 35 minutes on the lower rack of the oven. Remove and allow to cool on a grid.

Filling Preparation

Mix the mayonnaise, Dijon mustard, and the liquid honey together and stir in the chopped dill weed. Season with sea salt. Wash the apple, quarter it, and cut into thin slices. Cut the braided bread into slices and spread with the mustard sauce. Then cover with smoked salmon and apple slices and garnish with sprouts. Cover with another slice of braided bread. Repeat this process at will.

Christmas

LINGUINE CARBONARA

Ingredients

1 lb	Linguine pasta
2	Yellow onions
6 oz	Pancetta
4 Tbsp	Butter
4	Egg yolks
½ cup	Pecorino cheese, grated
½ cup	Parmesan cheese, grated
¼ cup	Parmesan cheese, shaved
	Salt & pepper from the mill

Preparation

Gently boil the linguine spaghetti to *al dente* in plenty of salted water. Peel and finely chop the onions. Cut the pancetta into fine strips and chop into small pieces. Melt the butter in a pan, add the onions and pancetta, and cook on low until onions are golden yellow.

In a large bowl, mix the egg yolks with the two cheeses and lots of pepper. Drain the spaghetti and promptly add to the egg yolk mixture in the bowl. Add the onions and pancetta. Mix all ingredients very quickly. Sprinkle again with pepper, salt to taste, and serve immediately.

Add a single raw egg yolk nestled in the midst of each serving for a special touch.

Christmas

DISHES ON THE SIDE

When it comes to Christmas dinner, the main course is the star of the show, but the side dishes make up an important supporting cast, especially when there are many guests at the Christmas banquet. Artfully pair your main course with sides that balance tastes and textures: smooth and crunchy, tart and sweet. Enhance the presentation of the meal with vibrant food colors and elegant serving plates. Side dishes can be like complementary presents filling the Christmas table with splendid bounty.

LEMON RICE

Ingredients

1 ½ cups	White rice
1 Tbsp	Olive oil
3 cups	Water
½ cup	Orange juice
1	Lemon, zested
	Sea salt

Preparation

Heat the olive oil in a saucepan. Add the rice and stir briefly. Add the orange juice and the lemon zest. Stir briefly and add the water and some salt. Boil the water, cover, and simmer gently for about 20 minutes. At the end, just before the rice finishes cooking, add a teaspoon of olive oil and stir in gently. Season with salt and serve.

CHAMPAGNE RISOTTO

Ingredients

2 cups	Carnaroli rice
3	Large shallots
1 Tbsp	Ghee clarified butter (or coconut oil)
1 cup	Champagne
3 ½ cups	Chicken stock
½ cup	Heavy cream

Preparation

Peel the shallots, cut them into tiny cubes, and braise them in ghee to a golden yellow. Add the rice, stir briefly with a wooden spoon, and pour in the champagne. Wait while stirring until the champagne is absorbed by the rice. Now add a ladle of chicken stock to the rice and let it boil over medium heat, stirring constantly. Repeat this process until the liquid is used up. Add the heavy cream and cover for about 5 minutes. Stir again and serve immediately.

POTATOES AU GRATIN

Ingredients

2 lbs	Russet potatoes
1 ½ cups	Heavy cream
1 cup	Whole milk
1 Tbsp	Butter
1 clove	Garlic
	Butter for greasing
	Sea salt

Preparation

Preheat oven to 250°. Peel and wash the potatoes and cut them into thin slices, less than ⅛ inch thick. Bring the cream, milk, and butter to a boil in a pot and add the garlic. Season with sea salt. Grease a gratin dish with butter. Layer the potato slices in the dish. Pour the prepared cream mixture evenly over the potatoes. Bake the potatoes gratin in the oven for about 2 hours.

POLENTA AU GRATIN

Ingredients

1 cup	Corn grits, coarse ground
1 cup	Water
½ cup	Hard butter
2	Egg yolks
½ cup	Parmesan cheese, grated
1 Tbsp	Thyme, chopped

Preparation

Preheat oven to 350°. Bring water to a boil with the butter, then add the grits and stir vigorously with a whisk until the grits are soft and swollen. Whisk and stir in the egg yolks and 1 tablespoon each of parmesan and thyme. Season with salt. Spread the grits evenly over parchment paper on a 9 x 12 baking sheet to cool for a bit. Separate the grits into portions with a mold or knife, sprinkle with the remaining Parmesan and bake until cheese is golden yellow, about 10–12 minutes. Serve the individual portions hot from the oven.

MASHED FLOURY POTATOES

Ingredients

2 lbs	Floury potatoes
½ cup	Butter
⅓ cup	Milk
¼ cup	Cream
	Salt
	Nutmeg

Preparation

Peel the potatoes and quarter them. Now put the potatoes in a saucepan, cover with water, and add 2 tablespoons of salt. Bring to a boil and cook to very soft, about 20–25 minutes. Drain the soft potatoes through a coarse sieve and let them evaporate for 10 minutes. Then return potatoes to the pot. Bring the milk and cream to a boil in a separate saucepan. Pour the hot liquid over the soft potatoes, add the butter, and stir vigorously with a whisk until the potatoes, butter, and cream have mixed smoothly.

Season to taste with salt and nutmeg.

Floury potatoes are richer in starch, with a cooked texture that is slightly flakey and very cohesive. With butter, salt, and pepper, these are ideal potatoes for mashing. Russet, Yukon Gold, and Majestic are among the best floury potatoes.

PEA MASHED POTATOES

Ingredients

3 ½ cups	Floury potatoes
1 ⅔ cups	Green peas
3 Tbsp	Butter
⅓ cup	Milk
¼ cup	Cream
1 Tbsp	Salt
	Sea salt for seasoning
	Nutmeg

Preparation

Peel the potatoes and halve or quarter them depending on size. Put the potatoes in a saucepan, cover with water, and add 1 tablespoon of salt. Bring the potatoes to a boil and cook until very soft, 25–30 minutes. Meanwhile, combine the peas with ⅓ cup milk and ¼ cup cream and boil softly until tender, then puree with a hand blender. Pour the soft potatoes and peas through a puree sieve and let them evaporate for 10 minutes.

Season with sea salt, pepper, and nutmeg, and serve warm.

POTATO BALLS

Ingredients

4 cups	Floury potatoes
2 Tbsp	Melted butter
1	Large egg
1 ½ Tbsp	Ground saffron
3	Shallots
1 Tbsp	Milk
4 Tbsp	Poppy seeds
	Sea salt

Preparation

Preheat oven to 390°. Cook the potatoes in a deep saucepan, peel them while hot, and press them through a puree sieve. Stir the milk into the potato mass. Beat the egg. Peel and finely chop the shallots. Stir the shallots, egg, saffron, and melted butter into the potato mixture and season with sea salt. Put the poppy seeds in a deep plate. Form approximately 30 balls from the potato mass and roll in the poppy seeds. Place on a baking sheet covered with parchment paper and bake in the middle of the oven for about 15 minutes.

BEET RISOTTO

Ingredients

2 cups	Carnaroli rice
1	Shallot
1 cup	Pinot Grigio wine
3 cups	Chicken stock
½ cup	Heavy cream
¼ cup	Beetroot juice
⅓ cup	Grated parmesan
	Olive oil for frying

Preparation

Peel the shallot, cut into the smallest cubes, and braise until golden in a saucepan with olive oil. Add the rice, stir briefly with a wooden spoon, and pour in the white wine. Wait while stirring until the white wine is absorbed by the rice. Now add a ladle of chicken stock to the rice and bring to a boil over medium heat, stirring constantly. Repeat this process until the liquid is used up. Now stir the cream and the beetroot juice into the risotto, remove from the heat, stir in the parmesan, then serve immediately.

What type of rice you use to make risotto is a most important factor in the taste and texture of any risotto dish. Carnaroli, known as the "king of Italian rices," is very high in starch content and makes for a thick and lush risotto. Beetroot juice is a welcome addition to this recipe, not just for the sweet and tart flavor, but also for the many beneficial health properties, including a boost to strength and stamina.

ROSEMARY POTATOES

Ingredients

1 ¼ lbs	New potatoes, close in size
2 Tbsp	Olive oil
1 ¾ tsp	Coarse sea salt
2 sprigs	Rosemary

Preparation

Preheat oven to 350°. Wash the potatoes well. Then pat dry. Halve the potatoes lengthwise. Pluck and chop the rosemary needles from the branch. Marinate the potatoes with rosemary, olive oil, and sea salt. After marinating, cook to soft in the oven for 35–40 minutes.

GERMAN POTATO SALAD

Ingredients

1 ½ lbs	New potatoes
4 cups	Shallots, chopped
2 ½ cups	Chicken stock
3 Tbsp	Herbal vinegar
5 Tbsp	Sunflower oil
	Salt & pepper from the mill

Preparation

Boil the potatoes, peel, and cut into fine slices. Finely chop the shallots. Place the chopped shallots in the pot with the broth and bring it to a boil. Once boiled, promptly pour over the warm potatoes. Add vinegar and oil and mix well. Finally, season to taste with salt and pepper, and serve warm. Refrigerate any remainder for serving later as cold potato salad.

POPPYSEED SPAETZLE

Ingredients

2 cups	Spelt white flour
3	Large eggs
½ cup	Whole milk
2 Tbsp	Butter
3 Tbsp	Ground poppy seeds
	Nutmeg
	Sea salt

Preparation

Beat the flour, poppy seeds, and eggs in a bowl with a wooden spoon. Gradually add the milk until the dough bubbles. Season with salt and nutmeg. Bring salt water to a boil in a saucepan. Press the dough through a spaetzle strainer or coarse colander into the boiling water. When the spaetzles rise to the surface, lift them from the water with a slotted spoon and put them in a sieve. Quench with cold water and drain well. Briefly sauté the spaetzles in a frying pan with butter. Set aside to cool briefly and serve.

Spelt is one of the oldest cultivated wheats, grown in the Near East as early as 5,000 BC In Greek mythology, spelt was said to be a gift from the gods, with its high fiber and protein content, and its rich, nutty taste. While spelt was an abundant and nutritious food staple from ancient times through the Middle Ages, it was supplanted thereafter by the more efficiently grown and processed common wheat. However, spelt has enjoyed a resurgence in recent years as a preferred specialty flour for artisan breads, cakes, and pastries.

NUDGE NOODLE

Ingredients

2 cups	Floury potatoes
¾ cup	White flour
3 Tbsp	Semolina flour
2 Tbsp	Clarified butter for frying
	Sea salt
	Nutmeg

Preparation

Cook and peel the potatoes the day before. The next day, press the potatoes through a ricer and mix with the other ingredients. Season with salt and nutmeg. Form the potato dough into a long roll and cut into small pieces. Shape the small pieces of dough into noodles, using the palms of your hands, and cook in salt water. Cool the finished noodles under cold water, pat dry, and fry in a pan with oil or clarified butter until golden brown. Season to taste with salt and nutmeg.

TRUFFLE RISOTTO

Ingredients

1 ½ cups	Carnaroli rice
3	Shallots
2 Tbsp	Olive oil
1 cup	White wine
4 cups	Chicken stock
½ cup	Heavy cream
1 ½ Tbsp	Truffle oil

Preparation

Peel the shallots, cut them into tiny cubes, and braise them in a saucepan in olive oil until they are golden yellow. Add the rice, stir briefly with a wooden spoon, and pour in the white wine. Stir until the white wine is absorbed by the rice. Once the wine has been absorbed, add the chicken stock about one cup at a time, over medium heat, stirring until the broth is brought to a boil. Repeat this process until the chicken stock is used up. Now add the heavy cream and the truffle oil and cover. Leave the rice to rest for about 5 minutes. Stir again and serve immediately.

RÖSTI

Ingredients

4 cups	Potatoes
4 Tbsp	Butter
	Ground nutmeg
	Salt & pepper from the mill

Preparation

Cook the potatoes the day before. Peel the potatoes and grate them on a rösti grater. Season with sea salt, pepper, and freshly grated nutmeg. Heat two tablespoons of butter in a pan and add the potatoes. Stir the potatoes with a wooden spoon until an even crust is formed. Fry them over medium heat for about 5 minutes, then slide the entire mass of rösti from the pan. Melt more butter in the pan, then flip the giant fritter, return it to the pan, and fry on low for 5 more minutes. Serve.

Rösti is a Swiss dish consisting mainly of potatoes in the style of a fritter. It was originally a breakfast dish, commonly eaten by farmers in the Bern region, but it is now enjoyed at any mealtime all over Switzerland and around the world. The French name röstis bernois pays tribute to its origin.

SAFFRON RISOTTO

Ingredients

2 cups	Risotto rice
3	Shallots
¼ cup	Butter, softened
1 cup	White wine
3 ½ cups	Chicken stock
¼ Tbsp	Saffron threads

Preparation

Peel the shallots, cut them into small cubes, and braise them in a saucepan in 1 ½ tablespoons of butter until golden yellow. Add the rice, stir briefly, and pour in the white wine. Wait while stirring until the white wine is absorbed by the rice. Stir the saffron threads under the rice. Now add a ladle of chicken stock to the rice and bring to a boil over medium heat, stirring constantly. Repeat this process until the chicken stock is used up. Stir the remaining butter into the risotto and serve immediately.

Christmas

THE JOY OF FONDUE

The origins of fondue are murky, but the Swiss Guard nonetheless prides it as a true Swiss dish. They say the recipe originated in rural lands in the 1700s where farm families made good use of a few cheese remnants, some stale bread, and a little wine, managing to conjure up a warm communal meal on a cold winter's night. Cheese fondue soon became hugely popular throughout Switzerland, but its popularity didn't spread until the Swiss Cheese Union mounted an advertising campaign in the 1930s to promote it worldwide. Fondue made a grand debut when it was served in the Swiss Pavilion at the New York World's Fair in 1964 and has been embraced across the Americas ever since.

VAUD FONDUE

Ingredients

1 clove	Garlic, halved
12 oz	Vaud's white wine
1 tsp	Lemon juice
1 ¾ lbs	Gruyère, grated
4 tsp	Corn starch
1 glass	Sherry
	Pepper
	Pinch of nutmeg

Preparation

Rub the *caquelon* (fondue pot) with the garlic clove. Mix the cheese with corn starch and bring to a simmer in the pot, together with white wine and lemon juice, stirring vigorously. Add the sherry and season with pepper and nutmeg.

FONDUE MOITIÉ-MOITIÉ

Ingredients

1 clove	Garlic, halved
1 ½ cups	White wine
1 tsp	lemon juice
1 ¾ cups	Gruyère cheese, grated
1 tsp	Corn starch
1 ¾ cups	Vacherin Fribourgeois, shredded fine
¾ cup	Sherry
1 pinch	Cayenne pepper

Preparation

Rub the fondue pot with the garlic clove. Mix the Gruyère cheese with corn starch and bring to a boil together with the white wine and lemon juice, stirring vigorously. Reduce the heat, add the Vacherin Fribourgeois and stir until it melts. The fondue must not cool beyond melting of the cheeses. Add the sherry and a pinch of cayenne pepper. Keep the fondue warm on the Rechaud.

Vacherin Fribourgeois is a semi-soft cheese made in west Switzerland. It has a firm texture and a fruity, aromatic taste. Genuine Vacherin is only made by a few artisanal cheese makers and hard to find. Fontina cheese is a good substitute.

The Rechaud is the classic fondue pot, a wrought iron, porcelain, or copper tabletop container and burner, essential for proper presentation and serving of fondue.

GENEVA FONDUE

Ingredients

2 ½ cups	Gruyère Cheese, grated
2 ½ cups	Raclette cheese, shredded
1 ½ cups	Emmantaler cheese, grated
1 ½ cups	White wine
1 tsp	Lemon juice
2 oz	Morel mushrooms, dried
1 Tbsp	Butter
4 tsp	Corn starch
½ cup	Marc brandy
	Pepper from the mill
	Nutmeg

Preparation

Soak the mushrooms in a little warm water. Meanwhile, mix all the cheeses with corn starch and bring to a boil together with the white wine and lemon juice, stirring vigorously. Then add the soaked mushrooms to the butter and add to the fondue with the marc just before serving. Season with pepper and nutmeg. Stir all gently and serve.

Marc (France) or grappa (Italy), is a fruit brandy made from pomace, the dregs left over from wine-making, after the grapes are pressed. Widely available in gourmet food and wine shops and on the Internet. There is no good substitute.

Instead of Morels, porcini mushrooms can also be used.

TILSIT RED FONDUE

Ingredients

2½ cups	Gruyère cheese, grated
2½ cups	Raclette cheese, grated
1½ cups	Emmentaler cheese, grated
1½ cups	White wine
1 tsp	Lemon juice
¼ cup	Morel mushrooms, dried (porcini mushrooms can also be used)
1 Tbsp	Butter
4 tsp	Corn starch
1 glass	Marc, pomace brandy
	Pepper
	Nutmeg

Preparation

Soak Morel mushrooms in water. Mix the cheese with corn starch. Add to fondue pot with white wine and lemon juice and bring to a boil, stirring vigorously throughout. Add the soaked Morel mushrooms (either whole or sliced) and the butter to the fondue. Add marc just before serving. Season with pepper and nutmeg and serve.

TOMATO FONDUE

Ingredients

2 Tbsp	Butter
1 clove	Garlic, pressed
1	Sweet onion, finely chopped
3	Tomatoes, *concassées*
1 cup	White wine
4 cups	Gruyère, grated
2 ½ cups	Emmentaler, grated
4 tsp	Corn starch
1 glass	Sherry
	Pepper
	Nutmeg
	Oregano
	Marjoram

Preparation

Put water in a pot to boil, and set aside a bowl of ice cold water. Prepare the *tomates concassées* by cutting out the eyes of the tomatoes and making criss-cross cuts at the base of each tomato. Add to boiling water for no more than a minute, then remove and submerge in the cold water. Peel off the tomato skins. Remove the seeds and cut the tomatoes into small cubes.

Melt the butter in the *caquelon*. Add the pressed garlic and onion and saute gently for a minute or two, then quench with white wine. Add the cheese and bring to a simmer on low heat, stirring constantly. Dissolve and add the corn starch, whisk in briskly, then add the sherry little by little. Continue to stir, bring to a simmer again, and season with pepper and nutmeg. Round off with sprinkles of marjoram or oregano.

Add tomatoes to the fondue at the very end of cooking, stir lightly, and serve.

> **Tomates concassées** *refers to tomatoes peeled, seeded, and chopped a specific way.*

Christmas with the Popes

POPE SAINT LEO THE GREAT
Christmas 451

Leo of Tuscany earned his place in history as St. Pope Leo the Great for many reasons. He was the defining pontiff of the Catholic Church in the first millennium, proclaiming the supreme authority of the bishop of the Church of Rome and defending the teaching of Jesus' two natures, divine and human, against heretical attack.

Pope Leo rose to legendary status for his confrontation with Attila the Hun, the ferocious warrior and conqueror of a wide swath of Asia and eastern Europe. Attila had turned his attention to the West, ravaging Gaul and northern Italy, and by 451, a confident Attila was charging down the peninsula, eager to plunder Rome for riches and treasure. These were the waning days of the Roman Empire, as war, famine, and plague had taken a heavy toll and the great city was virtually defenseless.

Many citizens were preparing to flee Rome when Pope Leo made a bold and courageous decision. He traveled north with an unarmed escort of bishops and priests to meet Attila, flanked by his entire army at the river Mincio.

After brief and formal greetings, the pope spoke plaintively to the grim monarch:

> Thou hast subdued, O Attila,
> the whole circle of the lands
> which it was granted to the
> Romans, victors over all peoples,
> to conquer. Now we pray that
> thou, who hast conquered
> others, shouldst conquer
> thyself. The people have felt
> thy scourge; now as suppliants
> they would feel thy mercy.

What happened next endures as a mystery of history. Suddenly, Attila withdrew his forces and turned back to the north, leading his army home without further engagement. Historians are at a loss to explain, but legend has it that higher forces were at play. Attila was said to have been shaken by a vision of St. Peter and St. Paul brandishing swords in the sky above.

The pope returned to Rome, hailed as hero. From that time on, he was known as Leo the Great.

Christmas was a joyful celebration at the Vatican that year. There had been scattered festivities in assorted places on December 25 since the date had been set by papal decree 100 years prior, but without more formal Church sanction, interest was fading.

Pope Leo was the first pontiff to step forward and proclaim the Good News and good reason to celebrate Christmas in one of his famous homilies:

> Our Savior, dearly beloved, was born today. Let us rejoice. For there is no proper place for sadness, when we celebrate the birthday of the Life, which destroys the fear of death and brings to us the joy of promised eternity.

For these few words, Leo the Great is called "The Pope Who Saved Christmas."

POPE GREGORY
Christmas 592

Gregorius was born into troubled times. The glory days of the Roman empire were long past, but his noble family still retained vast wealth and property, including a magnificent estate atop the Caelian Hill, one of the fabled Seven Hills of Rome. Gregory and his family were known as active and prominent Catholics, notable for two former popes in their ancestral line.

As a young man, Gregory was active in public life and rose quickly in rank. As chief administrator in Rome, he restored order and integrity to the city's finances. Acclaimed for his good character and many improvements in public welfare, Gregory was elevated to prefect of Rome before he was thirty years old. Soon after, he resigned and withdrew from public life, choosing a different path for his future.

Gregory converted the family estate to a monastery where he intended to live out his pious life in prayer and contemplation. But it was not to be. Gregory was summoned back to service, this time for the Church. Pope Pelagius II enlisted Gregory to act as his leading emissary to foreign heads of state and, later, as his closest adviser. When Pope Pelagius died suddenly in 590, Gregory was elected to succeed him despite his protestations and his longing to return to monastic life.

Gregory I served as pope for fourteen years and his record of benevolent works may remain unmatched. During a time of war, plagues, and the threat of famine, Pope Gregory orchestrated the re-direction of the abundant produce from thousands of acres of Church-owned farmland for distribution among the people of Rome.

Pope Gregory had many other accomplishments as well. An astute diplomat, he strengthened ties with bishops in distant lands to unify the Church. And it was Gregory who dispatched his friend, St. Augustine, and a group of monks to take the Good News of the Church to Britannia.

Christmas at the Vatican in 592 was a celebration of life and a tribute to Pope Gregory the Great. The beloved pope was declared a saint by popular acclaim upon his death in 604.

POPE BENEDICT XV
Christmas 1919

Six weeks after the beginning of World War I, Giacomo della Chiesa was elected pope. He led the Church through the difficult times of war and of the Spanish Flu in 1918–1919.

From the first days of his papacy, Benedict XV pressed for an end to the Great War, calling it the suicide of civilized Europe. However, his earnest appeals for peace fell on deaf ears. His ten-point plea for peace in 1917 was ignored by all leaders but was then used by Woodrow Wilson as framework for his own fourteen-point Peace Plan that led to the Treaty of Versailles.

The Spanish Flu flickered to life before the peace treaty was signed and roared to a blazing fire in weeks. Over the course of two years, the disease claimed the lives of an estimated 65 million worldwide, almost double the 34 million killed in World War I.

By papal decree, Pope Benedict unleashed the vast resources of the Church as the Spanish Flu reached pandemic status. The pope directed the cardinals and bishops of every diocese to offer Church schools and buildings as temporary hospitals and shelters. He sent an army of Catholic clergy to the front lines. Priests served as doctors and facilitators. Thousands of nuns became nurses in hospitals and emergency caregivers in poor neighborhoods. Many religious gave their lives to serve the sick. It was an unprecedented humanitarian effort.

The Spanish Flu waned suddenly in the fall of 1919. On Christmas Day of that year, Pope Benedict XV celebrated with a Mass of thanksgiving for God's grace and deliverance.

Three years later, there was a minor resurgence, a brief outbreak in and around Rome. Pope Benedict XV himself was one of the last casualties of the Spanish Flu. He died in 1922.

SAINT POPE JOHN PAUL II
Christmas 1981

It was one week after my swearing-in at the Courtyard of San Damaso as a member of the Pontifical Swiss Guard, on May 13, 1981, that my newly sworn solemn oath to protect the pope and the Church with my life was put to the test.

I was stationed at the Portone di Bronzo as thousands filed in for the weekly audience. When the Popemobile rolled into the square, the crowd surged to get close to their beloved John Paul II. Suddenly, a commotion near the pope and the sound of shots fired. I sprinted to the scene and helped as best I could. The moments were blurred and intense. The last I recall; we hurried the would-be assassin away from the enraged crowd to the small police office by the Portone while other Guardsmen raced the wounded pontiff to the hospital through the streets of Rome.

After the horrific event that played out before the world, service for those of us in the Guard was never the same. For 475 years, we had protected the life and safety of every Holy Pontiff, sometimes at the cost of many lives. But now, the unthinkable tragedy influenced everything at the Vatican, especially every aspect of security surrounding the pope.

For a time, the pope's life was in the balance, then there were months of arduous recovery. Even after his return to the

Vatican from the Gemelli Clinic in Rome, the pope had not regained his famous energy and strength. Weeks and months passed as summer followed spring. For John Paul II, it was a welcome time for the annual retreat to Castell Gandolfo. It was there that I had my brief personal encounter with the pontiff himself. He looked in my eyes and thanked me for my service and commitment, especially at St. Peter's Square on that dark day in May. How did he know? This was a moment that I will never forget.

With autumn came Advent, and Yuletide was upon us again and, with it, the days when a young Swiss Guard has wistful thoughts of home and family. Then came Christmas Eve. I had the special honor of serving as a Guard of the Throne during Midnight Mass. This is the most exalted position on the holiest night of the Christmas season, in the heart of venerable St. Peter's, and so close to the pope, only steps away.

It was the night when I witnessed the resurgence of the Holy Father. He was energized by the profound meaning of this night, and the faithful that surrounded him. It was a great joy for me to participate in this beautiful service.

Acriter et Fideliter,
Felix Geisser
Swiss Guard Emeritus

Christmas Desserts & Cookies

MAPLE CREAM CAKE

Ingredients

For the Dough

1 cup	Spelt white flour
⅓ cup	Raw cane sugar
⅓ cup	Butter
1	Large egg
1 tsp	Baking powder
1 cup	Dried peas, dried beans, or pie weights

For the Filling

1 ¾ cups	Heavy cream
½ cup	Maple syrup
5	Egg yolks
1 Tbsp	Corn starch

Preparation

Preheat oven to 390°. Grease a cake pan and set aside.

In a large bowl, thoroughly mix the flour and baking powder. Cut the butter into small pieces and add to the flour, along with the raw cane sugar and egg. Combine the ingredients with your hands until a pastry dough is formed. Line the greased pan with the pastry. Cover the dough with parchment paper, set the pie weights on top, and bake for 5 minutes. Then remove the weights and parchment paper and bake the dough for another 5 minutes. Reduce the oven temperature to 320°.

Stir the starch with 4 tablespoons of heavy cream. Add the maple syrup, the remaining cream, and the egg yolks. Mix well. Pour the mixture into the crust base and bake for 30 minutes. Allow the cake to cool until the topping is firm.

GINGERBREAD PLUM PARFAIT

Ingredients

6	Eggs
¼ cup	Honey
1 tsp	Cinnamon
1 tsp	Cardamom
5 slices	Gingerbread, diced (3 oz total)
4 cups	Whipping cream
7 oz	Dried plums
1 ½ Tbsp	Sugar
½ cup	Port wine
2 Tbsp	Rum
	Mint leaves for garnish

Preparation

Line a terrine mold or 4 small Timbale molds with clear cling wrap. Cut the crusts from the gingerbread slices and chop into small cubes. Beat the whipping cream until stiff peaks form. Beat the eggs to a creamy consistency in a double boiler and mix together with the honey, cinnamon, and cardamom.

Remove the bowl containing the egg mixture from the double boiler, place it in ice water, and stir briskly. Stir in the gingerbread cubes and fold in the whipped cream. Pour the mixture into the large mold or separate, smaller molds and place in the freezer overnight.

For the sauce, remove the cores from the dried plums and cut into fingernail-sized pieces. Marinate the pieces in the rum for about 1 hour. Bring the port wine to a boil with the sugar. Now add the rum with the plum pieces to the port wine. Simmer for 10 minutes and set aside to cool. To finish, pour the plum and port wine mix over the parfait. Garnish with mint and serve.

CLAFOUTI

Ingredients

3	Bartlett pears
1 ⅓ cups	Heavy cream
½ cup	Raw cane sugar
1 Tbsp	Vanilla extract
4	Eggs
1	Lemon, zested
1 pinch	Cinnamon
1 Tbsp	Brandy
1 pinch	Sea salt
½ cup	Spelt flour
¼ cup	Melted butter
	Extra butter for greasing

Preparation

Generously grease twelve 1-cup porcelain molds with butter. Preheat oven to 390°.

Wash the pears, peel and quarter them, and remove the core casings. Then cut the pears into thin slices and distribute the slices among the molds.

Combine all other ingredients except the flour and melted butter in a bowl and whisk until smooth. Gently introduce the flour into the mixture and combine well. Then slowly add the butter and stir thoroughly. Now ladle the mixture evenly into the molds. Place the molds on baking sheets and bake on the middle rack for 10 minutes. Reduce the temperature to 350° and bake for about 35 more minutes.

Remove from oven, let rest briefly, and serve warm.

CHOCOLATE CAKE SURPRISE

Ingredients

Serves 8

8 oz	Dark chocolate
¾ cup	Butter
1	Orange, zested
4	Eggs
½ cup	Powdered sugar
¼ cup	Flour
	Butter for greasing

Preparation

Cut the chocolate into coarse cubes. Using a double boiler, gently melt the chocolate and butter and combine with the orange zest. Whisk the eggs and place in the chocolate mixture, then add the powdered sugar and flour and mix gently but thoroughly. Place the mixture in the fridge for at least 4 hours.

Preheat oven to 350°. Coat 1-cup ramekins with butter and then dust them with flour. Carefully fill the molds with the chocolate mixture, place them on a baking sheet, and bake for about 12–14 minutes. Be careful not to overcook or you will lose the liquid center.

Serve right away on individual dessert plates.

CHEESECAKE DAVID

Ingredients

3 cups	Graham cracker crumbs
½ cup	Butter, softened
¾ cup	Quark (or low-fat cream cheese)
1 ⅔ cups	Sugar
2	Lemons, zested
6	Eggs

Crème Fraiche Topping

2 ½ cups	Crème fraiche
¼ cup	Sugar
1 tsp	Vanilla extract

Preparation

Preheat oven to 360°. Line the bottom of a 9-inch pie dish or a 9-inch springform pan with parchment paper. Put the graham cracker crumbs in a blender and reduce to very fine crumbles. Melt the butter in a saucepan and slowly mix in the graham cracker crumbs. Spread everything evenly into the baking dish. Bake on the bottom rack of the oven for 5 minutes.

In a mixing bowl, combine the quark, sugar, eggs, and lemon zest. Take the graham cracker crumbs out of the oven and slowly pour the quark mixture over the top of the crumbs. Return to the bottom rack of the oven and bake for 30 minutes. Turn off the oven and leave the baking dish inside for about an hour, or until a toothpick comes out dry. Remove and set aside to cool.

For the crème fraiche topping, preheat the oven to 425°. In a mixing bowl, combine the crème fraiche, sugar, and vanilla into a thick, even mixture. Pour evenly over the cheesecake and bake for 5 minutes.

The cheesecake can also be caramelized, if desired. To do this, cut the cheesecake into pieces, sprinkle with sugar, and caramelize with a kitchen torch until top is golden brown.

Christmas Desserts

DARK TOBLERONE MOUSSE

Ingredients

11 oz	Toblerone dark chocolate
2	Eggs
1 ½ Tbsp	Powdered sugar
1 ½ cups	Cream
1 ½ Tbsp	Bacardi rum
¼ cup	Chocolate chips

Preparation

Break the Toblerone into pieces and place in a bowl. Melt in a double boiler and add the Bacardi. Remove the bowl from the boiler and stir the chocolate until smooth. Beat the eggs and powdered sugar in a separate bowl until the mixture is light, then add to the melted chocolate, and mix well. Whisk the cream and carefully fold into the chocolate mixture. Refrigerate the mousse for 4–6 hours, until firm.

Serve in large dessert glasses, garnished with chocolate chips.

Christmas Desserts

PISTACHIO TORRONE

Ingredients

5 oz	La Florentine Pistachio Torrone
1 ¼ cups	Heavy cream
2 Tbsp	Pistachio liqueur
½ cup	Shelled pistachios
2	Figs
3 Tbsp	Fresh pomegranate seeds

Preparation

Chop the torrone to small morsels using a blender. Whisk the cream until stiff peaks form while adding the pistachio liqueur. Carefully fold the torrone pieces into the cream. Whisk gently to combine, then transfer to 4 ramekins. Set in the freezer for 30 minutes to firm.

Meanwhile, finely chop the pistachios and quarter the figs.

Before serving, dip the ramekins briefly in hot water, then slide out the contents onto individual plates. Decorate beautifully with the pistachios, figs, and pomegranate seeds.

CHOCOLATE ALMOND COOKIES

Ingredients

2 cups	Almond flour
2 cups	Powdered sugar
¾ cup	Dark chocolate powder
3	Egg whites
2 Tbsp	Sherry
1 tsp	Cinnamon
1 pinch	Ground cloves
⅓ cup	Turbinado sugar
1 Tbsp	Turbinado sugar for sprinkling

Preparation

Mix all ingredients with the egg whites. If the dough is too damp, add more almond flour. Set aside to rest for 1 hour.

Grease a baking sheet with butter and set aside. Sprinkle sugar on the table and roll the dough out to about a half-inch thickness. Use cookie cutters to cut the dough into heart, cross, and tree shapes. Place cookies ¾ inch apart on the buttered cookie sheet. Allow to sit at room temperature for one hour. Do not refrigerate. Preheat oven to 350°. Slide the sheet onto the highest rack in the oven and bake for about 5 minutes. The surface of the cookies should be slightly crusty but must not take on any color. After baking, leave on the cookie sheet for 2–3 minutes, then remove with a spatula and promptly place them into a tin or a plastic bag (for freezing). They must not be exposed to the air or they will harden quickly.

APRICOT JEWELS

Ingredients

½ cup	Butter, softened
¼ cup	Confectioner's sugar
1 tsp	Vanilla extract
½ pinch	Salt
½ of 1	Egg white
1 ½ cups	Flour
½ cup	Apricot jam
	Powdered sugar for dusting

Preparation

Mix the butter in a bowl. Add the confectioner's sugar, vanilla extract, and salt. Stir until the mixture is light and fluffy. Fold in the egg white. Add the flour to make a consistent dough and press the dough flat. Cover and set aside for at least 2 hours.

Preheat the oven to 390°. On a floured surface, roll the dough out to an ⅛-inch thickness. Use a cookie cutter to make rounds 1 ½ inches in diameter. Scoop out a small, round pocket in the middle of each cookie with a small spoon. Place cookies on baking sheets covered with parchment. Let sit for 15 minutes, then bake for 5–6 minutes in the middle of the oven.

Remove and cool the cookies on a cooling rack. Let the apricot jam warm briefly in a small frying pan, stir to smooth, then fill the pocket of each cookie. Dust all with confectioner's sugar. Serve warm.

Christmas Cookies

LEMON SUGAR COOKIES

Ingredients

1 ¼ cups	Sugar
4	Large eggs
4 cups	Flour, sifted
1 cup	Butter, softened
1 pinch	Salt
1 Tbsp	Grated lemon zest
2	Egg yolks for brushing

Preparation

Beat eggs with the sugar to a whitish cream. Add softened butter, salt, and sifted flour. Add the lemon zest. Whisk all to smooth. Leave the mix to rest for an hour.

Preheat oven to 325°. Butter a cookie pan. On a floured surface, flatten dough to a ¼-inch thickness with a rolling pin. Use cookie cutters to cut dough into preferred shapes. Place cookies on the buttered cookie sheet, brush with whisked egg yolks, and bake in the oven for 8–10 minutes. Check on the first batch often to make sure they don't brown. Serve warm or place in cookie tins. They can be stored for weeks.

CINNAMON STARS

Ingredients

2	Egg whites
1 ¼ cups	Sugar
1 Tbsp	Cinnamon
2 cups	Almond flour
1 Tbsp	Lemon juice
1 tsp	Lemon zest
	Sugar for rolling
	Butter for the tin

Preparation

Beat the egg whites, add the sugar and cinnamon, and stir until very smooth. Set aside 2 tablespoons of egg white for the glaze. Using a food processor, mix the rest of the egg white mixture with the almond flour, lemon juice, and lemon zest until it forms a dough. Leave to rest for 15 minutes.

Preheat oven to 390°. Sprinkle the table with sugar and roll out the dough to about a ½-inch thickness. Using star-shaped cookie cutters, cut out the cookies, place them on parchment paper, and brush the tops with the glaze. Set aside to rest for half an hour.

Slide the cookie sheets into the middle of the oven and bake for 6–8 minutes. Before removing them completely from the oven, turn the oven off, brush the tops with butter, and let them continue to sit for a minute or two on the middle rack, leaving the oven door open. Remove and allow the cinnamon stars to cool for a few more minutes and serve.

ANISETTES

Ingredients

3	Large eggs
2½ cups	Powdered sugar
1 Tbsp	Cherry or lemon juice
1 pinch	Salt
1 tsp	Anise
3½ cups	Flour, sifted

Preparation

Beat the eggs and sugar for 10 minutes, using a paddle stirrer, until creamy. Add anise, cherry or lemon juice, and salt. Fold the sifted flour into the mixture. Add more flour, if needed, so that the dough is firm enough to be shaped into balls. Cover the dough and set aside overnight.

The next morning, roll out the dough to about ⅜ inch thick. Place the small clay molds on top, press down, and cut off the dough all around. Flip the molds and gently press the dough into the molds by hand. Then use a dough knife to loosen the dough just a bit from each mold and trim the edges.

Place the anisettes on the greased baking sheet and let them sit at room temperature for 24 hours. The sheets must not be placed on top of each other so that they are able to rise.

Preheat oven to 320°. Bake the anisettes for 15 minutes, making sure not to overcook them or let them take on color. The underside should not be browned either.

After baking, this pastry is hard. To make it soft and tender, leave them out, uncovered, in an airy place for 3–4 days. Then place them in a sealed cookie tin and wait at least 2 weeks before serving.

HAZELNUT COOKIES

Ingredients

3	Egg whites, large
1 pinch	Salt
⅓ cup	Sugar
2 cups	Hazelnuts, ground
50	Whole hazelnuts, shelled

Preparation

Cover baking sheets with parchment paper and set aside. Beat the egg whites until stiff peaks form. Add the salt and half the sugar. Beat until the egg white mixture has a glossy sheen, or shines. Fold in the ground hazelnuts with the remaining sugar. Place the dough in a pastry bag with a serrated spout (⅜-inch diameter).

Squeeze 40–50 small mounds onto the covered cookie sheets. Add 1 hazelnut to each mound, pressing slightly into each cookie. Leave the cookies uncovered at room temperature for at least 6 hours or overnight. Preheat the oven to 350°. Bake for 10–11 minutes in the middle of the oven. Move the cookies from the baking sheet to a platter or cookie tin. Serve at your pleasure.

SABLES

Ingredients

Makes about 40 cookies

1 cup	Butter, softened
½ cup	Sugar
2 tsp	Vanilla extract
1 pinch	Salt
3 cups	Flour, sifted
	Sugar for rolling
1/2 cup	Milk

Preparation

Mix butter with a stirring paddle until creamy. Add the sugar, vanilla extract, and salt, and continue stirring until the mixture is smooth and light. Sift the flour and mix briefly to form dough. Knead the dough and add milk a tablespoon at a time, if needed, to make the dough soft and pliant. Add milk sparingly, no more than 1/2 cup at most. Sprinkle the work surface with sugar and shape the dough into 4 rolls, about 1½ inches in diameter. Wrap each roll with cling wrap and refrigerate for 3 hours.

Cover a large baking sheet with parchment paper. Remove the prepared rolls from the refrigerator, cut into ½-inch thick slices and place on the baking sheet. Refrigerate for about 30 minutes.

Preheat the oven to 400°. Bake the cookies on the center rack of the oven for 10–12 minutes. Watch carefully so they don't brown. Remove and set aside to cool briefly. Serve warm.

AMARETTI

Ingredients

Makes 50 cookies

3 ½ cups	Powdered sugar
3 ½ cups	Almond flour, blanched
4	Egg whites, large
2–3 drops	Bitter almond essence

Preparation

Line two baking sheets with parchment paper. Place the egg whites in a large mixing bowl and beat until soft peaks form. Fold in the powdered sugar, almond flour, and bitter almond essence and mix well with a hand blender. Dampen your hands in order to form the dough into 50 walnut-sized balls. Place them onto the baking sheets evenly spaced apart. Pinch the balls at the top with fingertips. Set aside to rest in a cool place for at least 5 hours.

Preheat oven to 375°. Bake one sheet at a time on the middle rack for 22–24 minutes. Allow to cool on the sheets. Gently remove amaretti from the parchment and dust with powdered sugar.

VANILLA ALMOND COOKIES

Ingredients

1 ¾ cups	Flour
1 cup	Almond flour, blanched
¾ cup	Confectioner's sugar
1 tsp	Vanilla extract
1 pinch	Salt
1 cup	Cold butter, cut into pieces
1	Egg, large (whisked)

Preparation

Mix the flour, almond flour, sugar, vanilla extract, and salt together in a mixing bowl. Incorporate the butter into the flour mixture by hand until it forms a crumbly mass. Add the whisked egg and mix into a thick dough. Roll the dough flat, cover, and let sit for 2 hours in a cool place.

Line 2 baking sheets with parchment paper. Shape the dough into finger rolls. Cut each roll lengthwise into strips, ¾ inch in width. Cut the long strips into 2-inch pieces and shape each piece into a small croissant. Place on the 2 baking sheets and set aside for 15 minutes.

Preheat the oven to 325°. Bake both sheets simultaneously. After 10 minutes, switch the sheets, placing the top sheet on the lower rack and the lower sheet on the higher rack. Bake for 10 more minutes to cook evenly. Remove, let cool, dust the cookies with sugar, and serve.

CHRISTMAS PRAYERS AND GRACES

Let the just rejoice, for their justifier is born.
Let the sick and infirm rejoice, for their savior is born.
Let the captives rejoice, for their Redeemer is born.
Let slaves rejoice, for their Master is born.
Let free men rejoice, for their Liberator is born.
Let all Christians rejoice, for Jesus Christ is born.

— St. Augustine of Hippo

At the birth of Our Lord the angels sing in joy: Glory to God in the highest, and they
proclaim peace to men of good will as they see the heavenly Jerusalem being built from
all the nations of the world. When the angels on high are so exultant at this marvelous
work of God's goodness, what joy should it not bring to the lowly hearts of men?

— Pope Saint Leo the Great

Your mercy reaches from the heavens through the clouds to the earth below.
You have come to us as a small child, but you have brought us the greatest
of all gifts, the gift of eternal love. Caress us with Your tiny hands, embrace
us with Your tiny arms, and pierce our hearts with Your soft, sweet cries.

— St. Bernard of Clairvaux

O sweet Child of Bethlehem, grant that we may share with all our hearts in this profound mystery of Christmas. Put into the hearts of men and women this peace for which they sometimes seek so desperately and which you alone can give to them. Help them to know one another better, and to live as brothers and sisters, children of the same Father. Reveal to them also your beauty, holiness, and purity. Awaken in their hearts love and gratitude for your infinite goodness. Join them all together in your love. And give us your heavenly peace. Amen.

— **Saint Pope John XXIII**

Christmas Around the World

ARGENTINA
Feliz Navidad

Like many places, Argentina celebrates the Christmas season by stringing lights, hanging wreaths, and decorating trees. Most homes place a crèche, or pesebre, right beside their Christmas tree in honor of the season's true meaning, the Nativity of Christ. However, unlike the Christmases in the Vatican, those in Argentina are distinctly warm!

For most Argentinians, the season's main event is Christmas Eve. Many Catholics attend a Vigil Mass in the afternoon as a way of beginning the holiday festivities that can last far into the night.

In these festivities, the main meal is served late, often after 11 p.m. The warm weather allows the Christmas Eve dinner to be a barbecue, with turkey, pork, and goat being among the most popular entrees. For appetizers, canapes navideños are favorites. These are small, open-faced empanadas with a variety of fillings, including meats and cheeses, fruits and vegetables, and herbs and spices. The traditional Christmas desserts are pannetone and pan dulce, delectable Argentinan pastries.

The late festivities are the Argentinian way of hailing Christmas morning with good food and cheerful celebrations. At midnight, many will set off fireworks or release paper lanterns into the sky. It is truly a merry occasion!

Wish each other a merry Christmas in Spanish by saying Feliz Navidad!

EGYPT
Eid Milad Majid

S ince the time of Joseph, and Moses before him, Egypt has played a significant role in biblical history. After Jesus was born, the Holy Family fled to Egypt to escape the evils of Herod, whose soldiers were already pursuing the Christ Child.

There are more than nine million Christians in Egypt today. Many are Coptic Christians, with an ancient history of their own. Egyptian children call Santa Claus Baba Noël, meaning Father Christmas, and set out kahk, sugar cookies stuffed with honey, nuts, and dates, in the hopes that he will visit their homes and leave gifts.

Wish each other a merry Christmas in Arabic by saying Eid Milac Majid!

THE PHILIPPINES
Maligayang Pasko

Christianity came to the Philippines in the sixteenth century with the arrival of Spanish and Portuguese explorers. Colonists, merchants, and clergy soon followed. Today, the islands make up the most intensely Christian nation in all of Asia, with 80 percent of the 100 million inhabitants identifying as Catholic.

For Filipinos, the Christmas season is the most important time of the year and it does not end until the spectacular Feast of the Black Nazarene on January 9. The feast day makes up one of the largest holiday fests in the world, with millions crowding the streets of Manila for the religious procession and day-long celebration.

The iconic wood statue portrays a black Jesus struggling under the weight of His cross. It was donated to the Philippines in the seventeenth century by an unknown sculptor and soon after took on mystical status. Many believe that the statue has miraculous healing power, capable of curing diseases and answering urgent prayers upon contact with it. As the parade moves through the streets of the capital, devotees press in from all sides, straining to touch the cross or kiss the foot of the Black Nazarene. Thousands walk the entire four-mile route barefoot as a sign of penance and respect.

To wish each other a merry Christmas, Filipinos say in Tagalog, Maligayang Pasko!

SWITZERLAND
Schöni Wiehnachte

anta Claus, or Samichlaus, is known to arrive in Switzerland every year on December 6 for Samichlaus Abend, or Santa Night. Together with his hooded companion, Schmutzli, Samichlaus lives somewhere in the great Swiss forest, only emerging at Christmastime to bring gifts and treats to homes throughout the land.

Samichlaus is a typical version of Santa, jolly and benevolent, dressed in red robes trimmed in white, with a long, white beard. Although, instead of using a sleigh and reindeer, Samichlaus arrives on a donkey, laden with sacks of gifts for the good children.

Schmutzli, on the other hand, is a different story; he is far from the typical happy elvish helper. Rather, he acts as the darker alter-ego of Samichlaus, there to set misbehaved children straight. Scary in appearance, dressed in black, with a dark beard and a scowl on his face, he walks around carrying a broomstick instead of a sack of gifts.

As the tradition goes, Samichlaus and his helper arrive through the front door and the children get to receive their treats from him right away!

Wish each other a merry Christmas in Swiss German by saying Schöni Wiehnachte!

FONDUE CHINOISE

Ingredients

2 lbs	Assorted meats (beef tips, veal fillet, and pork fillet)
6 cups	Beef bouillon
2 cups	Chopped vegetables (onions, carrots, leeks, and celery)
1	Bay leaf
1	Clove
2 sprigs	Thyme leaves
2 Tbsp	Cognac
	Salt & pepper from the mill

Preparation

Bring the bouillon with bay leaf, cloves, and thyme to a boil in a saucepan on the stove. Turn off the flame and let it steep for 15 minutes. During this time, cut the meat into bite-sized pieces and cut the vegetables into small cubes. If the bouillon has cooled, pour it through a sieve into a Rechaud pan and bring to a boil again briefly. Then place the pan on the table and light the Rechaud burner. Use the fondue forks to add the meat pieces to the pan a few at a time. Cook for a minute or two, depending on how you like it.

For another good meal: After eating, add the leftover chunks of vegetables to the remaining bouillon and chill overnight. The next day, add the cognac, heat to a soft simmer, and serve in soup mugs.

DUCK WITH CRANBERRY SAUCE

Ingredients

4	Duck breasts (4 oz each)
2 Tbsp	Cranberries, dried
1 cup	Red port wine
¼ cup	Red wine
1 cup	Chicken broth
¼ cup	Heavy cream
2 pinches	Ground ginger
1 pinch	Cocoa powder
1 pinch	Cardamom, finely ground
1 tsp	Corn starch
	Salt & pepper from the mill

Preparation

Cut the duck breasts into diamond shapes. On the skin side, season with sea salt, pepper, ginger, cocoa, and cardamom. On the meat side, season with only salt and pepper.

Preheat oven to 175°. Place the breasts with the skin side down in a dry frying pan, and fry the skin until crispy brown. Then flip and fry the meat side brown as well. Put the breasts in a deep dish in the oven and cook for about 45–50 minutes. Make sure to repeatedly remove the excess duck oil and fats from the dish with a baster.

Add the port wine and red wine to the frying pan and reduce by half over high heat. Pour in the chicken stock and add the dried cranberries. Reduce by a quarter and add the cream. Bring to a boil again briefly and bind with corn starch, if necessary.

Use a meat thermometer to make sure the duck reaches an interior temperature of 160°. When it does, take the duck breasts out of the oven and slice them thinly. Arrange on individual plates and pour the cranberry sauce over them. Serve proudly, with extra sauce in a gravy bowl.

SPINACH POTATO GNOCCHI

Ingredients

9 oz	Spinach leaves
10 oz	Floury potatoes (like Russets)
1 cup	Flour
1	Egg
1	Egg yolk
1/3 cup	Parmesan, grated
3 Tbsp	Butter, softened
	Salt and pepper
	Nutmeg for sprinkling

Preparation

Cook and peel the potatoes the day before. The next day, press the potatoes through a potato press or coarse sieve. Blanch the spinach, quench it in ice water, mix and squeeze for juice; should be about 1/3 cup. Add the green spinach juice to the potato mass. Now add the remaining Ingredients, except the butter, and process everything into a dough.

Form the potato mass on a work surface and shape into long sausages and cut every ¾ inch. Pinch the edges of gnocchi together lightly. Cook the potato gnocchi in boiling salt water. As soon as they swim and float to surface, take out with a slotted spoon and quench in cold water.

The finished gnocchi can now be fried to a golden brown in a buttered pan, about 3–5 minutes. Sprinkle with the Parmesan, season to taste with salt, pepper, and nutmeg, and serve warm.

RABBIT MEZZE

Ingredients

Makes about 24 pieces

For the Ricotta Dough

1½ cups	White flour
½ cup	Butter
¾ cup	Ricotta cheese
1 tsp	Sea salt

For the Filling

½ lb	Minced rabbit (best from the flank)
3 Tbsp	Toasted bread crumbs, finely grated
¼ cup	Heavy cream
2 Tbsp	Chicken stock
2 tsp	Grappa (or any fruity brandy)
1	Onion
1	Orange, zested
1	Egg yolk
	Olive oil for frying
	Cinnamon, to taste
	Cardamom, to taste
	Salt & pepper from the mill

Preparation

Mix the flour with the salt in a bowl. Cut the butter into small cubes and add to the flour. Mix the flour and butter with your hands so that the dough becomes crumbly. Add the ricotta and mix until smooth. Flatten the dough and chill for about 30 minutes. Then roll out the dough on a floured work surface, to about a ¼-inch thickness. Use a round cookie cutter with a 3-inch diameter to cut out pieces of dough.

Finely chop the onion and braise in olive oil until golden. Now mix the onions with the toasted bread, the cream, and the rabbit meat. Then add the orange zest, sea salt, pepper, cinnamon, and cardamom and mix. Heat a little olive oil in a pan and briefly fry the rabbit mixture in it. Then deglaze with grappa, pour in the stock, and let simmer.

Preheat oven to 350°. Place the egg yolk in a small container and set aside.

Spread the rabbit mass over the center of the circles and fold up the dough. Press the edges to seal the dumplings, using your fingers or a fork. Brush the dumplings with the egg yolk and bake for 25 minutes on the middle rack of the oven until golden. Serve.

FAJITAS ARGENTINE

Ingredients

For the Tortillas

½ cup	White flour
⅓ cup	Corn flour
½ tsp	Baking powder
½ tsp	Sea salt
⅓ cup	Water
1 Tbsp	Olive oil
	Olive oil for frying

For the Filling

1 lb	Chicken breast, shaved
1	Pepper
1	Zucchini
2	Roma tomatoes
2	Spring onions
1 cup	Corn kernels
2	Avocados
1	Lime
½ cup	Cilantro leaves
¾ cup	Crème fraiche or sour cream
⅓ cup	Mayonnaise
1 ¾ cups	Mozzarella cheese, shredded
⅔ cup	Reggianito cheese, grated
2 Tbsp	Olive oil for frying
	Salt and pepper

Preparation

Put the white flour, corn flour, baking powder, and salt in a bowl. Add the water and mix to a smooth dough. Add the olive oil, knead briefly, and leave to rest for 30 minutes. Then, with a wood rolling pin, carefully form the dough into thin, round tortillas. Put a little olive oil in a crepe pan and make about 5 tortillas in it. Flip the tortilla when the dough becomes firm. Of course, ready-made tortillas are always an option.

Preheat the oven to 350°. Wash the vegetables. Remove the pepper casing and seeds and cut into thin strips. Cut the zucchini into thin sticks. Remove the tomato quarters, remove the core casing, and cut into small cubes. Cut the spring onions into thin strips. Halve the avocados, remove the stone, and crush using a fork. Season with lime juice, sea salt, and pepper. Sprinkle the pepper and zucchini strips with a little olive oil. Season the chicken meat with sea salt and pepper and fry in olive oil. Mix with the peppers and zucchini. Place in the oven for 15 minutes.

Meanwhile, spread the corn, tomatoes, avocado, spring onions, cilantro, crème fraiche, mayonnaise, mozzarella, and Reggianito cheeses in small bowls. Remove the meat and vegetables from the oven, set them on the table, and fill the tortillas as you like.

Couscous Salad Ingredients

1 ½ cups	Couscous	1 Tbsp	Pine nuts
12	Cherry tomatoes	1 Tbsp	Sesame seeds
1	Cucumber	2 Tbsp	Argan oil
15	Olives, pitted	½ tsp	Baharat
1 Tbsp	Pistachios, chopped		

TAJINE BEEF & COUSCOUS SALAD

Ingredients for Tajine Beef

¾ lb	Beef shoulder
3	Onions, finely diced
2 cloves	Garlic, finely diced
¾ cup	Prunes
2	Red chili peppers
3	Roma tomatoes
1 tsp	Harissa
1 pinch	Cardamom
1 pinch	Nutmeg
1 cup	Vegetable stock
3 Tbsp	Olive oil
1 tsp	Paprika
¼ tsp	Cinnamon
	Salt & pepper from the mill
	Mint leaves for garnish

Dressing Ingredients

5	Mint leaves
1 bunch	Parsley
1 clove	Garlic
6 Tbsp	Olive oil
2 Tbsp	Water
1	Lemon (juice & zest)
1 bunch	Spring onions

Tajine Preparation

Wash the meat, pat dry, and cut into strips. Peel the onions and garlic cloves and cut into small cubes. Halve the chili peppers lengthwise, core, wash, and cut into fine strips. Cut several small slits in the tomatoes with a pointed knife and briefly add them to boiling water. Then quench the tomatoes cold, skin, and core. Cut the tomato pulp into small cubes. Heat the olive oil in a frying pan and fry the onions and garlic briefly in it. Add the meat and tomatoes and fry briefly. Then add the spices and chili peppers. Add half of the vegetable broth and simmer over a low heat for about 40 minutes. Add the prunes and the remaining vegetable broth and cook for another 30 minutes over a low heat. Garnish with the mint leaves.

Salad Preparation

Make the dressing by chopping the mint leaves and parsley together. Press the garlic clove. Halve the spring onion and cut into fine rings. Mix the olive oil, water, and lemon juice. Add the mint, parsley, lemon zest, garlic, and spring onion. Season with salt, pepper, turmeric, and cumin.

Bring 1 cup of water to a boil and pour over the couscous. Leave to cool briefly. Loosen gently with a fork. Roast the pine nuts in a dry frying pan to a golden brown. Cut the cherry tomatoes in sixths. Halve the cucumber, remove the seeds, and cut into small cubes. Quarter the olives. Mix all ingredients with the couscous and marinate with the dressing. Keep the mix loose and fluffy. Season with sea salt and pepper and garnish with the pistachios and pine nuts.

Epiphany

"WHERE IS HE WHO
HAS BEEN BORN KING
OF THE JEWS?"

–MATTHEW 2:2

*I*n less than 300 words, the Gospel of Matthew tells the story of the Three Wise Men who travel from distant lands, following the bright star to seek out the newborn Messiah. There is intrigue and suspense as they come upon the child Jesus in the arms of his mother, as well as a happy ending as the Magi foil the evil plans of Herod and return by dark passage to their homelands to spread the good news.

GOSPEL OF MATTHEW
CHAPTER 2, VERSES 1–12

After Jesus was born in Bethlehem in Judea, during the time of King Herod, Magi from the east came to Jerusalem and asked, "Where is the one who has been born king of the Jews? We saw his star when it rose and have come to worship him."

When King Herod heard this he was disturbed, and all Jerusalem with him. When he had called together all the people's chief priests and teachers of the law, he asked them where the Messiah was to be born.

"In Bethlehem in Judea," they replied, "for this is what the prophet has written: 'But you, Bethlehem, in the land of Judah, are by no means least among the rulers of Judah; for out of you will come a ruler who will shepherd my people Israel.'"

Then Herod called the Magi secretly and found out from them the exact time the star had appeared. He sent them to Bethlehem and said, "Go and search carefully for the child. As soon as you find him, report to me, so that I too may go and worship him."

After they had heard the king, they went on their way, and the star they had seen when it rose went ahead of them until it stopped over the place where the child was. When they saw the star, they were overjoyed.

On coming to the house, they saw the child with his mother Mary, and they bowed down and worshiped him. Then they opened their treasures and presented him with gifts of gold, frankincense, and myrrh.

And having been warned in a dream not to go back to Herod, they returned to their country by another route.

THE THREE WISE MEN
Gaspar, Melchior, and Balthasar

Historians, scientists, and biblical scholars have scoured the records and searched the stars in a relentless quest to answer the many questions about the Three Wise Men that have persevered through the ages.

Who were they?

We still don't know for certain. For 500 years, the Magi remained anonymous. First mention of the names Gaspar, Melchior, and Balthasar in Christian literature emerged in the sixth century and became part of the legend, without foundation in the Bible or in historical records.

Where were they from?

The consensus is that Persia and Mesopotamia were likely homelands of the Magi, though some suggest areas in and around Syria or Saudi Arabia, even as far as India.

Were they kings?

Despite the Christmas carols, it is far more likely that they were wise and respected noblemen, royal advisors perhaps, but not kings.

Were they present at the Nativity?

The ubiquitous presence of the Magi in crèches and Nativity art is contradicted by the passage in Matthew that clearly states they arrived at a "house," not a stable, and found a "young child," not an infant. There are other indications in historical records that the Magi may have only begun their long trek when Jesus was born and thus arrived months later.

DAL

Ingredients

1 Tbsp	Sesame oil
2 tsp	Cumin
1 tsp	Fennel seeds
1	Onion, diced
1 clove	Garlic, diced
1	Chili pepper
¾ cups	Red lentils
3 cups	Water
3 tsp	Garam Masala spice blend
2 tsp	Curry
	Sea salt

Preparation

Peel and dice the onions and garlic. Heat the sesame oil and toast the cumin and fennel seeds. Add the onions and garlic and let them tighten briefly. Wash the chili pepper, halve, remove the core casing, and cut into thin strips. Add the lentils with the sliced chili pepper and top up with water. Add the spices and simmer for about an hour over low heat. Stir from time to time. Season with sea salt only after the cooking has ended.

Dal is a dried, split legume dish served as a solid food or a thick soup. It is ubiquitous across the Indian subcontinent, available in myriad varieties. Dal is among the most important food staples in South Asian countries.

Epiphany

TAJINE LAMB

Ingredients

1 lb	Leg of lamb meat
2	Onions
¼ lb	Tomatoes
⅓ lb	Russet potatoes
1 cup	Chickpeas from the can, drained
2 Tbsp	Olive oil
1 ¼ Tbsp	Argan oil
1 ½ tsp	Cumin
1 tsp	Paprika
½ tsp	*Ras el Hanout*
1 cup	Water
	Salt & pepper from the mill

Preparation

Cut the meat into ¾-inch cubes. Peel and dice the onions finely. Wash the tomatoes, cut into eighths, and remove the white skins and seeds. Peel the potatoes and cut into ½-inch cubes. Put the chickpeas in a colander, rinse them with cold water, and let them drain. Heat the olive oil in a saucepan and braise the onions in it. Add the meat and stir-fry briefly. Sprinkle the Ras el Hanout over the meat and continue to fry briefly. Season with sea salt and pepper. Then add the chickpeas, tomatoes, and potatoes and pour a cup of water over them. Cover the ingredients and heat at medium for 20 minutes. Simmer, stirring occasionally. Finally, add the Argan oil and, if desired, season again with the spices, salt, and pepper. Serve.

The colorful containers are as old as the recipe, and are also called "Tajines"

Epiphany

FALAFEL

Ingredients

For the Falafel

1 ¾ cups	Chickpeas, from the can, drained	1 Tbsp	Olive oil for cooking
1	Onion, small	2 Tbsp	Breadcrumbs
1 clove	Garlic	½ tsp	Bahrat spice
½ cup	Parsley, chopped	2 Tbsp	Oil for frying
½ cup	Cilantro, chopped		Fresh ground salt & pepper

For the Red Beet Hummus

2 ½ cups	Chickpeas, soaked for 12 hours		Olive oil
2 Tbsp	Tahini (sesame paste)	2 Tbsp	Cumin
2	Lemons, juiced	1 tsp	Turmeric
4 cloves	Garlic, pressed	2 pinches	Spinach powder
½ cup	Parsley, chopped	1 pinch	Paprika
		1 Tbsp	Red beet juice (or water)
			Fresh ground salt & pepper

Falafel Preparation

Peel the onion and garlic and cut into small cubes. Add both to chickpeas and mix together. Add the parsley, cilantro, olive oil, and breadcrumbs, and mix all to a smooth consistency with a food processor. Season with Bahrat spice, sea salt, and pepper. Form falafel balls from this mass. Heat the frying oil and fry the falafels to a warm golden color. Lift out with a slotted spoon and drain on paper towels.

Hummus Preparation

Drain the water from the soaked chickpeas, then simmer the chickpeas in unsalted water for about 40 minutes.

Drain, then finely puree the chickpeas with a blender. Add some red beet juice (or water) until there is a creamy consistency. Mix with tahini, lemon juice, pressed garlic, chopped parsley, olive oil, cumin, and turmeric and season with salt, pepper, and paprika powder. Cool for 30 minutes.

For nice color accents, add a few dashes of spinach powder and sprinkle the red beet juice onto hummus. Mix in well. Use beet-colored hummus as nest for falafel balls.

ABOUT THE AUTHORS

David Geisser

David Geisser was born and raised in the Wetzikon district of Zurich, Switzerland. David already was an accomplished young chef and published author when he enlisted in the Pontifical Swiss Guard in 2013. He was honored to serve under the 266th Supreme Pontiff of the Church of Rome, Pope Francis. Today, David is one of the leading chefs in Switzerland, author or co-author of seven cookbooks, host of his own TV show, and the founder and leader of the David Geisser Cooking Studio. David and his wife, Selina, reside in Zurich today.

Thomas Kelly

Thomas Kelly is not a chef, not even a good cook, but he is a veteran writer, author, journalist, editor, and producer. Kelly is the author, co-author, or editor of more than a dozen books in various genres and has worked extensively in radio, television, and movies. He lives in Cleveland, Ohio with his wife, Anne.

This is the second collaboration between David Geisser and Thomas Kelly. They were co-authors (with Erwin Niederberger) of *The Vatican Cookbook*, a national bestseller published in 2016.

A NOTE OF THANKS

There were so many valuable contributors to the creation of this cookbook. While we cannot thank them all, we would like to acknowledge the special contributions of:

Kelly Amen

Michael Canty

Gina Marie Criscione

Parnell Egan

Margaret Gallagher

Felix Geisser

Gerry Grim

Timothy Carlisle Kelly

Richard Morris

Glenn O'Brien

John O'Brien

Sean Cardinal O'Malley

Dan O'Shannon

Elaine Simmons

Andreas Widmer

Tom Wilson

The Holy See of the Vatican City State

The Pontifical Swiss Guard

PHOTOGRAPHY END NOTES

- THE SILVERWARE CHRISTMAS TREE is a playful and spirited composition of photographer Liliya Kandrashevich. [Page X]

- SWISS SOLDIERS CROSS THE ALPS is an illustration from the Luzerner Schilling (Lucerne chronicle), a sixteenth-century illuminated manuscript that chronicles the history of the Swiss Confederation, written by Diebold Schilling the Younger of Lucerne. [Page 4]

- THE ROYAL CHRISTMAS TREE is admired by Queen Victoria, Prince Albert, and their children. It wasn't until Germany's Prince Albert introduced the Christmas tree to his new wife, England's Queen Victoria, in 1841 that the tradition was established in England. [Page 38]

- STAINED GLASS NATIVITY is from the Cathedral of St. Michael and St. Gudula in Brussels, Belgium. The window was an eighteenth-century addition to the 800-year old church. [Pages 68–69: Photograph by Jorisvo]

- MEETING OF LEO THE GREAT & ATTILA THE HUN is a magnificent fresco painted by Raphael in the sixteenth century and located in the Apostolic Palace of the Vatican. [Page 97: Photograph by Viacheslav Lopatin]

- CEILING OF THE HALL OF CONSTANTINE was located in one of the great rooms of the Raphael Stanze but is now located in the Vatican Museums. It was painted by Raphael and his assistants in the early 1500s. Many believe that Raphael considered this work to be a response to Michelangelo's Sistine Chapel. Raphael died before its completion. [Pages 100–101: Photograph by Viacheslav Lopatin]

- FESTIVAL OF THE BLACK NAZARENE is the single biggest annual religious celebration in the world, taking place in the capital of the Philippines, Manila. Millions attend the parade of the revered statue of a black Jesus each year on January 9. [Page 148: Photograph by Shadow 216]

PHOTOGRAPHY CREDITS

Superb photography is an inherent part of *The Vatican Christmas Cookbook,* and we are grateful for the contributions of the finest photographers from Rome, Switzerland, the United States, and elsewhere.

The principal photographer and provider of all food photographs is **Roy Matter** of Zurich, Switzerland. Roy Matter is a food photographer, food biologist, and an accomplished chef himself. Roy Matter and David Geisser have collaborated on three best-selling cookbooks and many other projects. For Roy Matter, his photography work is food art, which is as much a part of the experience as the food itself.

Additional credits

Riccardo De Luca: Swiss Guard Marches to Urbi and Orbi (VIII)

Liliya Kandrashevich: Abstract Christmas Tree Made from Cutlery (X)

Courtesy Selina Geisser: David Geisser and Pope Francis, et. al. (XI)

Renata Sedmakova: The Prophets by Leopold Bruckner (2)

Warren Bouton: Advent candles glow and mark the celebration of Christmas/Advent Wreath (3)

5PH: Hot Barley Soup (6)

Alexander Donchev: Saint Nicholas (12)

Louis Jean Desprez: King Gustav III Attending Christmas Mass in 1783, in St Peter's, Rome; Nationalmuseum, public domain (26–27)

Art Heritage/Alamy Stock Photo: Domenico Ghirlandaio, Nativity (30)

Anonymous: Royal Christmas tree 1848 (38)

Valerio Mei: Nativity in St. Peter's Square (48)

L'Osservatore Romano: Pope kissing baby Jesus, pope addressing the crowd in St. Peter's Square (48)

Luca Prizia/Pacific Press/Alamy Live News: Vatican City. Annual Holy Mass of Christmas Eve at St. Peter's Basilica in Vatican City, Rome, December 2014 (50)

Yulia Kotina: Pope Francis greets the pilgrims during his weekly general audience in St Peter's Square, January 2014 (62)

Riccardo De Luca: Vatican City, December 25, 2018. Swiss Guard line up in St. Peter's Square before the Pope Francis' Urbi et Orbi Christmas Day blessing from the central loggia of St. Peter's Basilica (64–65)

jorisvo: Stained Glass Window Nativity Scene, Cathedral of Brussels (68–69)

AM113: Vatican City, Nativity Scene and the Christmas tree in St. Peter's Square (82–83)

Francesco Solimena: The Meeting of Pope Leo and Attila (97)

Courtesy Felix Geisser: Felix Geisser Swearing In (102)

Courtesy Felix Geisser: Felix Geisser & John Paul II (102)

L'Osservatore Romano/ Swiss Guard: Pope John Paul II wounded (103)

Master Francke: Birth of Jesus (143)

Orhan Cam: Main Gate of the Hanging Church (El Muallaqa) in Coptic Cairo, Egypt (147)

Millenius: Christmas Ornament with Flag of Argentina (146)

Will Rodrigues: La Casa Rosada (The Pink House) is the executive mansion and office of the president of Argentina, in Buenos Aires (146)

Renata Sedmakova: The Flight to Egypt (147)

AGCreations: Middle Eastern cookies (147)

at.rma: Christmas parol/lantern with graphics of baby Jesus, Mary, and Joseph (148)

Shadow216: Feast of The Black Nazarene in Manila, Philippines (148)

Dotshock: Zermatt Valley and Matterhorn Peak, Switzerland (149)

Sailko: Carlo dolci, Italian Baroque paintings in the National Gallery, London (164)

The Picture Art Collection / Alamy Stock Photo: Henry Siddons Mowbray, *The Magi* (166)

Riccardo De Luca: Vatican City, June 9, 2019. A Swiss Guard attends the Pentecost Mass celebrated by Pope Francis in St. Peter's Square (175)

About
SOPHIA INSTITUTE

Sophia Institute is a nonprofit institution that seeks to nurture the spiritual, moral, and cultural life of souls and to spread the Gospel of Christ in conformity with the authentic teachings of the Roman Catholic Church.

Sophia Institute Press fulfills this mission by offering translations, reprints, and new publications that afford readers a rich source of the enduring wisdom of mankind.

Sophia Institute also operates the popular online resource CatholicExchange.com. Catholic Exchange provides world news from a Catholic perspective as well as daily devotionals and articles that will help readers to grow in holiness and live a life consistent with the teachings of the Church.

In 2013, Sophia Institute launched Sophia Institute for Teachers to renew and rebuild Catholic culture through service to Catholic education. With the goal of nurturing the spiritual, moral, and cultural life of souls, and an abiding respect for the role and work of teachers, we strive to provide materials and programs that are at once enlightening to the mind and ennobling to the heart; faithful and complete, as well as useful and practical.

Sophia Institute gratefully recognizes the Solidarity Association for preserving and encouraging the growth of our apostolate over the course of many years. Without their generous and timely support, this book would not be in your hands.

www.SophiaInstitute.com
www.CatholicExchange.com
www.SophiaInstituteforTeachers.org

Sophia Institute Press® is a registered trademark of Sophia Institute.
Sophia Institute is a tax-exempt institution as defined by the
Internal Revenue Code, Section 501(c)(3). Tax ID 22-2548708.